WHAT I CAN DO

What I Can Do

Mary K Hoodhood
Lisa McNeilley, PhD

LAKESHORE LITERARY

CONTENTS

This is the story of Mary K. Hoodhood as she remembers it. Memory is a crazy thing, so there's a chance others might remember the same events differently. That's okay, because the underlying truth remains the same. The people in Mary K.'s life are real, and she has been guided by a deep respect for all of them when including them in her story. But some of them are mentioned by relationship without being named, and some are mentioned by first name only.

WHAT I CAN DO

Published by Lakeshore One, an imprint of Lakeshore Literary, Inc., 1590 44th St SW, Wyoming MI 49509.

www.lakeshoreliterary.com | +1 616 606 0966 | @lakeshore_lit

Cover/jacket design and illustration by Abby Holcomb. Cover photograph by Adobe Stock. Mary K. Hoodhood photograph by Michael Buck. Lisa McNeilley photograph by Trudi Smith.

ISBN-13: 978-1-943548-40-8 (hardcover)
        978-1-943548-41-5 (softcover)
        978-1-943548-42-2 (ebook)

Library of Congress Control Number: 2022945982

First Edition: January 2023

Printed in the United States of America.

FROM MARY K. TO JEFF:

This book is dedicated to you, just as I am dedicated to you. My life is possible because of your love and devotion. Even when I call you an idiot, I am forever in love, and I treasure every minute we spend together.

———

FROM LISA:

To Dave, your love and support allowed me the freedom to take on this project and dedicate my time to writing, so I am dedicating this book, the results of my efforts, to you with love and gratitude for giving me the chance to do what I love.

*To Mary K., it seems silly to dedicate this book to you because it is **your** book. You are living this life, but you trusted me to tell your story, to put your thoughts and experiences into words, and I am truly grateful.*

FOREWORD
By Rev. George K. Heartwell

I first met Mary K. when I was wrestling with a career decision, one that ultimately carried me from business to ministry among the homeless. I needed to do something that would put me in touch with people in need. While I was still working in mortgage banking and driving for Capitol Lunch (later renamed God's Kitchen), I thought volunteering to deliver meals to homebound low-income seniors seemed like a safe way to put a toe in that water. The voice on the other end of the line when I called to inquire if drivers were needed was confident, encouraging, and (yes!) inspiring. That voice belonged to Mary K. Hoodhood. Picking up my meals for delivery, I met this strong, confident lady and was totally surprised to find her in a wheelchair.

Later, when I was planning an immersion experience living among the homeless for a week, Mary K. was one of a handful of people whose counsel I sought. Before she would bless my venture, she had to make sure my heart was right.

What I found in Mary K. was such a deep love for the people on the margins of society that she needed to know that I would do or say nothing that would in any way deny their dignity.

Mary K., Jeff, and George Heartwell.

Career wise Mary K. and I were never far from one another. I assumed a role as pastor of Heartside Ministry and we shared the geography of the Heartside Neighborhood, each in our own way providing care for the homeless men and women (and sometimes children) who found themselves on the street. More often than not we would see each other across social services planning tables sharing ideas about new approaches to care for the homeless and marginalized people of Grand Rapids. When I took a new role in local elected office, Mary K.'s strong voice of advocacy for the disenfranchised became a North Star for me as I attempted to navigate stormy political waters. Always—at every stage of my relationship with Mary K.—I found her to be a source of inspiration.

Joseph Campbell, the American literary giant and philosopher wrote, "We must let go of the life we have planned, so as to accept the one that is waiting for us." True enough; and many of us understand this statement existentially. But what happens when the life you had planned is suddenly wrenched from your grasp? What happens when one who has been raised in an active life—sailing, biking, skiing—suddenly, inexplicably, but permanently, finds herself without use of arms and legs? Plans dashed on the rocky shoal, how easy it would be to enter a state of perpetual despair, to imagine that no bright future "is waiting for us."

This is Mary K.'s story, and the way in which she shaped a future for herself out of disability is amazing. You will read about relationships that changed her life. You will see the role that faith played in sustaining her through hope. You will roll with her from paralysis to a life so active it will make you gasp!

And you will be inspired! Just like her first intern was. I still remember the conversation with Bridget Clark that initiated a connection that has spanned two decades.

"George, I've gone through this whole list of internship sites and none of them inspires me! What am I going to do?" Bridget asked.

Bridget was in her third year at Aquinas College in

Grand Rapids, majoring in Community Leadership. Professor Mike Williams and I were co-teaching the courses. Third year students take a 20 hour per week internship with a Grand Rapids area nonprofit or governmental organization. I arranged the internship sites and I thought they were all amazing. Bridget didn't like anything I was offering!

After I saw Mary K. at an event and she told me what she was working on, I called Bridget and said, "Inspiration? You want inspiration, Bridget? I'll give you inspiration! Call this lady: Mary K. Hoodhood."

Mary K. had just launched her pilot project out of God's Kitchen, providing sack suppers for 125 children in three Grand Rapids Public elementary schools. She hadn't even given the project a name yet. It was the start of Kids' Food Basket, an organization that was the culmination of Mary K.'s expertise and dedication to serving others. I knew that if anyone could inspire Bridget, it would be Mary K.

Mary K. had created something unique and wonderful that, at this writing, provides approximately 1.4 million meals a year to children in West Michigan and other communities.

Inspiration? Mary K. Hoodhood is the very definition of the word. But to inspire others, she first had to inspire herself, which she did after a traumatic accident that caused a spinal cord injury that would have broken a lesser person. In the pages that follow you will hear Mary K.'s story of trial, grit, and lifelong resolve. What you won't hear is self-pity. If she ever had those dark thoughts, she surmounted them, and quickly! She found her purpose in serving others in the way that she could...not with her body, but with her keen mind and her abiding passion for the common good.

The other thing you won't hear is self-aggrandizement. Mary K. is too humble to brag on herself.

That's my job!

I know first-hand the impact that this remarkable individual has had on my life; and I have heard so many people say, "Mary K. has a 'presence'. There's just something about her. Something magnetic that draws you to her." Perhaps, dear reader, you are one of those who have encountered Mary K. at a low point in your own life and been inspired by her resilience, her brilliance, and her perseverance against all odds. If you have not been so fortunate, I suspect that, by the time you finish reading this book, you will look at your own life in a new and positive way. You will be inspired.

There's just something about her...

The Rev. George K. Heartwell was mayor of Grand Rapids,
Michigan, from 2004 to 2015.

PEACE COMES FROM WITHIN

I have to stop this cascade of memories, or at least take them out of their drawer only for a moment, have a brief look, and put them back. I know how to do it now: I have to take the key to acting and apply it to my life. There is no other way to survive except to be in the moment. Just as my accident and its aftermath caused me to redefine what a hero is, I've had to take a hard look at what it means to live as fully as possible in the present.

— *CHRISTOPHER REEVE*

I woke up and it felt like I had entered a void. I could hear the beeping of machines around me and the sound of hushed voices. I realized that I was moving, that I was lying in a bed that was turning back and forth, right 90 degrees, flat, then left 90 degrees in slow motion, though it was still dizzying. There were people in the room with me and I could turn my head from side to side to see them, though they were just blurred outlines at first. I wanted to call out, but my mouth was blocked with tubes. The world seemed hazy and confusing, and I couldn't figure out where I was or what was happening.

Mary K. and Jeff.

Pieces of time came back to me in little flashes. I remembered Jeff packing up the Volkswagen Beetle with his tools, our tent, and other supplies. I remembered the drive to Silver Lake Sand Dunes where we were going camping. Jeff called us "The Three Amigos," me, him, and his six-year-old daughter, Melisa. We were excited and happy to be taking this trip together, and even though Jeff and I had only known each other for just over a year, there was no doubt in my mind that we were a family. We set off on the long car ride with Mel sleeping on my lap, Jeff driving. I dozed off a little myself, and then woke when Jeff said, "Look, we're almost there. You can see the dunes." I turned my head to look. A flash of color, a loud crash. The car swerved.

Then there was nothing.

No time, no place, no memory. It was like staring into a black screen after the movie has ended. There were little murmurs of static, just the tiniest wisps of memory, but they were absorbed by the blackness.

The feeling in my body was like a throbbing numbness, like when your foot falls asleep and you can't shake it to get the blood flowing again. The sensation was difficult to pinpoint, as though the numbness was the physical version of constantly hearing a buzzing sound, a persistent annoyance that was not exactly pain but felt relentless.

The room was disorienting as I flipped slowly from viewing one side to another. I was on a ventilator, and would be for ten days, and the whoosh of air going in and out of my lungs formed a steady rhythm, accompanied by the beeping of machines I couldn't identify. Finally, my mother's face appeared, a look that reflected joy and fear and hope as she called out to the nurse, "She's awake, she's awake!"

The quiet comfort of knowing my mother had been at my bedside calmed me a little in these inexplicable circumstances. I didn't know what was happening to me, but I knew my mother could handle anything, would handle anything, and therefore, so could I. Another flip, and I realized Jeff wasn't there. A new fear for Jeff and Mel overtook anything I was feeling for myself. I knew without doubt that Jeff would be with me if he could. If he wasn't here, there was a reason. I couldn't speak because of the ventilator, but I think my mom must have known what I needed to hear.

"He's alive. He's still at Hackley Hospital in Muskegon. You were airlifted to Grand Rapids Blodgett." She didn't tell me anything else. I clung to the thought that as soon as he could, Jeff would be with me. I knew he would not give up on me.

The nurse checked on the machines that were keeping me alive, and I felt so much gratitude for her, for the machines, for the little bit of blue sky I could see through my window. I was still groggy, and it felt like some weird dream was happening that I couldn't quite grasp.

Then the doctor came and stopped my bed from rotating while he was talking, which a relief. He explained what had happened and what they had done to save me. We had been in a car accident, and I had been crushed inside the car after it rolled several times. The doctor said I had suffered a spinal cord injury at my C4-C5 vertebrae. He said I had been in a coma for two days. Two days? Two days. The loss of those two days hit me, but it was nothing like the loss unfolding before me.

I would be paralyzed for the rest of my life.

I heard the words he was saying, but it was almost as if they didn't have meaning. I couldn't grasp the situation, couldn't believe this was happening to me, couldn't fully understand what it meant. My first thought was that this couldn't be real—there was no way this could be *my* life. That sense of the surreal made me feel almost disassociated from myself. There was the me who was the person I had always been, and there was the me who was the person in this bed. I kept thinking that there had to be some way to get back to that old me, the real me, to the real life I was supposed to live. If it just required a force of will, I knew I had that. If it was a matter of going back and undoing that one moment, I would figure out a way to do that.

Somewhere deep down I knew none of that was possible, but I wasn't ready to face it yet. I think I was in shock. I would try to grasp the reality of the situation, but either my own mind or the drugs they were giving me would take over and it couldn't quite sink in. Eventually, the details wormed their way into my brain, but it would take a long time for them to settle in. I didn't know it in those first days, but ahead of me lay months of managing changing emotions and years of learning how to direct my mind toward the positive side of things, no matter what.

I could see my mother crying behind the doctor, but I kept telling myself, "At least I'm alive." I firmly believed that where there is life, there is hope, and I wasn't ready to give up hope yet. That would have meant giving up not only on myself, but on the value of life itself. Like trying on a new dress to see how it fits, I tried on this new version of my life by repeating to myself what the doctor had said. I would be paralyzed with feeling from my chest up, but nothing below that. I had the ability to move my head and my shoulders. When I got out of the hospital bed, it would be to sit in a wheelchair. It still wouldn't quite register that this was really happening, that this would be my life.

The doctor turned the bed back on and I resumed my rotation from side to side. The movement was slow, almost meditative. I knew I was moving because I could see my view of the room change from side to side. In my chest, head, and shoulders, I still had feeling, so as my weight shifted, I could feel the pull of gravity first one way then the other, even though I was strapped into the bed. It was like some strange scene from a horror movie, but it was me, my life. I thought about what the doctor said, and I knew it must be true, but it still wasn't registering. I couldn't put together the words he said and see how they applied to me. My brain was still trying to work it out.

I had so many questions. Was there a chance I could get better? What would my life be like after this? Would I be able to do anything for myself? If I couldn't walk again, what would I do? Where would I live? How would I live? Why was this happening to me? I couldn't talk so these questions were unvoiced. I was locked inside a body that wouldn't move and a mouth that couldn't speak.

If they gave me the answers, I couldn't remember. I just tried to be calm and waited for Jeff. For the next couple days, my mother watched over me with my sister and brothers taking shifts with her. My family—Mom, Joanne, Tom, Dave, Mike, and Terry—had decided that I would never be left alone and set up a 24-hour rotation. They watched over me, a belated form of protection, which was wonderfully comforting. I knew that even if Jeff wasn't there, he would come for me, even though nobody would let me know how he and Mel were doing. I knew they were in the car with me and had been injured, but not how badly. For some reason, the doctors thought it was better to leave it to my imagination rather than to tell me the facts. My mind swung between despair and hope as I was flipped from side to side in that ceaselessly moving bed. How would I live from now on? I knew that Jeff would never leave me, but I still worried. How would I live with this even if I had Jeff? We had gotten engaged, planned a life together, a life full of the things we loved, like camping, and travel, days at the beach, nights dancing under the stars. It wasn't fair.

————

After I spent two more days in the hospital, Jeff burst into my room. He was okay, and Mel was okay. She had been released from the hospital after having at least 50 stitches. She had stitches in her knee and on her eyebrow, eventually leaving her with a scar in almost the same spot as one of mine. I was so relieved that she hadn't suffered permanent injuries. If her head had been struck just two inches higher, she would have had a head injury and might still be in the hospital like me. Instead, she was with her mother.

Jeff told me how it happened. He talked and walked from one side of the room to the other so I could see him as I was flipped back and forth, captive of the Rota-Rest bed.

Memorial Day weekend was the busiest weekend of the year at the dunes. Lines of cars stretched along the single lane heading west, with just a few coming in the other direction. As Jeff was driving, a seven-year-old boy, he found out later, ran across the street to get the mail from the row of mailboxes there. Jeff said he could see the boy smiling as he ran into the front right quarter panel of the car without looking. Jeff swerved, but there was no time, the boy hit the car and rolled up into the windshield before being thrown onto the pavement. When Jeff realized he was facing oncoming traffic, he used all his strength to pull back into the lane to avoid hitting vehicles that might be coming at us from the other side of a hill. The car rolled. Jeff threw himself across the dashboard to try to take the force of the impact and protect Mel and me. The car rolled again. Jeff was thrown through the windshield. Mel was thrown from the vehicle. The car rolled a third time with just me in it. For Jeff, everything went black, and he didn't know how much time passed after that.

Someone gave Jeff smelling salts and he woke up lying on the pavement with a pain in his abdomen and with his blood gushing onto the roadside. Mel was there, hurt but safe. An officer hovered over Jeff asking if he had been drinking or speeding or if there were drugs in the car. The cop was looking for an answer—how could there be such death and destruction without a discernible cause? For years we wrestled with the same questions. How could bad things happen to good people? How could such devastating consequences come when we had done nothing wrong? How could there be no one and nothing to blame? Why did this happen to us? How could a little boy be dead?

Lying on the side of the road with the police officer questioning him, Jeff didn't have time to think of those things. That would come later. He looked around and couldn't see me, and it hadn't occurred to the officer that there might have been someone else in the vehicle. Jeff used the front of the officer's shirt to pull him down to his level and yelled, "Why are you asking me this? Where's my fiancée? Get my family to a hospital now!" Jeff gathered his strength and stood, searching for me along the side of the road, along with a couple of other officers. The car was a crushed orange ball of steel, and nobody thought it would even be possible for a person to be trapped inside, so they searched the area instead.

This was a time before seat belts were widely used. There were no booster seats for Mel. There was no annoying beeping to make you wear a seatbelt. No laws, not even a general awareness that they were needed—almost nobody I knew even thought about seat belts. It was natural to assume I had been thrown from the car. After looking and calling for a couple of minutes along the road, as a last resort, Jeff staggered over to the car, braced his foot against the side and pulled the mangled passenger door until he ripped it open. My arm fell out, dangling over the side of the wreckage, and they realized I was still inside. Each successive roll of the car crumpled the metal shell tighter around me until I was left with nothing but a tiny air pocket.

Jeff said it felt like forever before emergency personnel started to arrive, including the ambulance and fire department. It took them over two hours to cut me out of the Volkswagen Beetle, and by that time an airlift had arrived to take me to the hospital. If I had been conscious, I would have been crying for Jeff and Mel, who were taken by ambulance without me. I would have been terrified about what was happening to me. Or maybe I would have enjoyed the majestic view of the dunes with Lake Michigan beyond, but I have no memory of those moments.

When the helicopter arrived at Hackley Hospital, according to Jeff, the doctors took one look at me and said there was no way a small-town hospital like theirs had the resources to keep me alive through the night. So, there was another airlift, to Blodgett Hospital in Grand Rapids, where there was a little bit of hope, but only a little, of keeping me alive. The hospital room I ended up in there would be my home for months.

The doctors had kept Jeff and Mel at Hackley Hospital, miles away from me, recovering from stitches and all the injuries they sustained. The nurses and doctors wouldn't tell him what had happened to me, and there were times when he believed I hadn't survived. But when his parents finally told him I was at Blodgett and had woken up, he decided he had to come to see me. A nurse came into his room to find him taking the IV out of his arm.

"You aren't strong enough to leave yet. We expect you to be here for at least ten days, and you haven't even had four days to recover."

"I have to see my fiancée. I need to see Mary K.," Jeff told them. "If you would just tell me how she is, I could face it. I've already had to deal with one death. Can't you see how I feel?" The nurse brought in the doctor.

"If you can stand up, get dressed and walk out of the room, I'll discharge you," the doctor told him, fully expecting Jeff to be unable to even move. He had been living with the death of that young boy. Jeff told me he had been living with the fear of another death, mine, and the thought that he couldn't live without me, so he gathered up his strength and stood up beside his bed. He used his arm to brace himself on the bed for a moment because he was too dizzy to walk. After a minute, he knew he could walk, so he got dressed and the doctors discharged him, though they were pretty unhappy about it. He went with his parents to their house, got a car, and came directly to me.

When Jeff walked into my hospital room, I was still strapped in the bed, being turned from side to side.

"Mary," he said, "I'm so sorry."

I couldn't say anything, but tears were streaming down my face. That's when I learned what it was like to cry and be unable to wipe away the tears or blow my own nose.

There was a part of me that realized how awful this was, that felt grief and sorrow for the boy's family and their terrible loss. But I was still in a state where everything seemed unreal, as though I was watching a movie rather than living a life. So, there was a part of me that just wasn't accepting what was happening. At this point, that was the biggest part. I was just so happy to see Jeff, so relieved that he and Mel were okay, that I'm not sure if my tears were tears of sorrow or of joy. I didn't realize at the time how deeply this sorrow, guilt, and fear would seep into our lives. It would take years of talking together, of processing what happened, of trying to make amends to the world. Jeff suffered a form of PTSD, reliving the accident over and over, waking in the night screaming from nightmares. At those times, I wondered who was suffering most, him or me. As Mel grew up and our grandson JJ was born and grew happy and healthy, both Jeff and I would think of that little boy and his family. The loss was so great that sometimes it was unfathomable. We would remember him for a lifetime and for each milestone that Mel or later JJ experienced, we would hold him in our hearts as well.

———

When I was taken off the ventilator and could finally speak, I said, "I knew you would come." My voice was raspy from disuse and from the irritation of the tubes, but it was such a relief to talk, to have at least this restored to me.

Jeff stayed in the hospital with me from that first day to the last. He sat with my mother or my siblings or other friends and family when they came. He was recovering from serious injuries himself and from a broken heart over the death of a young boy. He told me that part of him died that day, too. Rationally, we knew there was nothing that could have been done, that we weren't at fault, that we had just been in the car that happened to be there the moment he ran into the street. But humans aren't rational. We grieved for him and his family and felt the weight of his death. Even after Jeff was cleared of any wrongdoing, we grieved.

One time when we were alone, Jeff stopped the bed from rotating and said to me, "I killed a boy. He ran into our car, and he died." I knew him so well, and I knew what that had done to him. We cried, with him holding my hand, his face pressed against my chest. I could feel the pressure and warmth in that one small part of my body. It felt like pain and comfort at the same time. Then he wiped away my tears and his own, and we stayed together, wondering how we would build a future out of this wreckage, but knowing we would have to find a way.

Together we would heal, both physically and emotionally, though healing didn't mean that I would walk or regain full use of my arms. Healing didn't mean that we would

WHAT I CAN DO

forget. Healing meant simply that we would figure out how life was going to be. Jeff wanted to start that life together by getting married on the spot. He went to the chapel to find a priest, he called his church, he asked anybody he could think of, but nobody would agree to marry us.

"When you blow this popsicle stand, we're going to get married and buy a house," Jeff said. I pictured our dream house and thought about decorating it. Thought about what we would do on the weekends Mel came to stay with us, and the family we would invite over, and the meals we would have. There was a life to look forward to. I had to make myself believe that.

I knew that the dream life I thought I would live wasn't going to be. I would have to find a new dream. I didn't know what that was going to look like, but I knew I had to figure it out. I had always believed that an intelligent, resourceful person could solve a problem. I had this one life, and I wasn't willing to live it without joy and love. I would find a way. It's one thing to think that life is precious and that as long as you are alive, you are worth fighting for, that there is always hope. It's another thing to know it so deep in your soul that you take action and build a life. I sometimes wonder if I hadn't been injured if I would have been so conscious of the choices I had. Somehow, narrowing the field created a focus, first on staying alive, and later on making that simple act, something that most people take for granted, meaningful.

As Jeff used to say, "You only have two choices in life. You can either pass or fail. It's that simple." I did not intend to fail. I also knew that I would need help. It's true that none of us can get through life without the help of family, friends, and community, but I found myself in a place that pushed this truth to the ultimate. I was totally vulnerable and totally dependent on others. But I was not unarmed in this fight. I had my intelligence, my humor, my compassion, and my ability to love the people in my life.

And I felt loved. My mother's love, that of my family, Jeff's love. I felt the strength my dad had passed on to me, even though he was gone now. I looked at the walls, covered with hundreds of cards from people who wished me well. I asked, "Can you take the cards down and show them to me?" but nobody seemed to have the time, or maybe reading those messages just felt like coming too close to admitting the truth about my injuries for my mom. I wanted to see who they were, these people who were hoping for me to heal, these people who cared. It felt good knowing they were out there, and when I left the hospital, the cards came with me. When I was finally able, I had my attendant read each one to me. Many of those people had visited me in the hospital, but these messages showed me that I was in the hearts of even those who weren't able to be present. This feeling of loving and being loved sustained me throughout my rehabilitation. It gave me hope. Since I was going to be totally vulnerable and dependent on others, love made the world feel less threatening. That didn't mean that accepting help was going to be easy.

One Sunday afternoon in the hospital, my mom came into the room, and it was just the two of us. I had been thinking about my life, and I started crying. This was the first time reality had finally settled into my mind. I had a sense of what my life was going to be moving forward. All the things I couldn't quite believe were true. I would be paralyzed, vulnerable, unable to do the things I thought I would do, dependent on everyone around me.

"What's wrong?" she asked. I know that sounds like a crazy question because so much was wrong, but I knew what she meant. She had seen me through the weeks of adapting, and she knew my strength. In this moment, there was something uniquely wrong, and my mom just wanted to give me a chance to talk about it.

"I'm just sad that you and Jeff are going to have to do everything to take care of me."

"It will be all right." I knew she meant it, but my new life was going to involve a huge change, from an independent woman having fun to a person needing someone else to wipe my nose and give me every sip of water. I didn't have a choice, though, so there would have to be a way for me to become all right. I had nobody to talk to who knew exactly what I was going through. My family and friends could love me and offer support. Jeff could stand by me. But the truth was I only had myself and the strength I could pull from some inner depths. I just kept telling myself that I had no choice.

Still, I rue that day. A nurse saw me crying and decided I must be depressed. She had me prescribed antidepressants. I tried to tell the doctors that I wasn't depressed—I was just upset and dealing with the situation I found myself in. There's a difference. They didn't listen. The next week was awful. I told them the drugs were not sitting right with me. I felt even more groggy, and everything was hazy. I couldn't think clearly or put together a sentence to talk to my family. One of the greatest challenges when you have an issue or disease is getting drugs at the right level, not too strong or too weak, that actually help you. In the fog of uncertainty, it can be difficult to communicate your needs and it can be difficult for medical professionals to truly understand or change the course of treatment. I was able to get them to stop the meds only by insisting.

Part of this is our attitude toward suffering. We think that feeling bad is bad in and of itself, something to be avoided at all costs. But there are times in life that warrant feeling bad. Sometimes suffering is necessary. We need to be present with the suffering and bear the weight of the sorrow and grief and fear in our bones, let them go through us, know they are a part of us, a part of being human, and then we need to fight our way out from under that sorrowful load to find something else—acceptance, peace, a new way to find happiness.

———

After a month, I was told I had to have another surgery. I had a spinal fusion in which they took a piece of my hip and put it in my neck to strengthen my neck where it was broken. My recovery from that was more lying in that bed, flipping from side to side, fighting off grief and fear. I had to have a ventilator again for a couple of days, so I couldn't communicate. When my family thought I was sleeping, I was often lying there with my eyes closed, giving myself some space. Much of the time I was praying, and I found strength in my faith. I had been raised with the knowledge that all life was valuable and meaningful, and God was merciful. My Catholic upbringing was based on the principle that "human life is sacred and that the dignity of the human person is the foundation of a moral vision for society. This belief is the foundation of all the principles of our social teaching." I took this precept to mean that since I was alive my life had meaning and value. I would find a way to make my own life sacred but also to contribute to the sanctity of the lives around me.

Without control of my body to create change in the world and to direct my life, I would have to rely solely on what I could accomplish with my soul, with my willpower, with my brain. If I reached deep inside myself, I could find the coping skills I needed, and I wouldn't give up. They were within my grasp because of the way I was raised, because of my spiritual strength, because I was blessed with a temperament that would help me be optimistic and courageous.

In those moments alone in my thoughts, I decided three things. First, and most important, I would not let myself be deterred from finding purpose and happiness. Second, I would not drive away the people I love by becoming someone drowning in self-pity. I had known some complainers who nobody wanted to be around. I wouldn't become like them, even though I might have a lot to complain about. Third, I would not allow myself to dwell on the things I couldn't do but would find the things that I could do and focus on them. I might remember fondly the feeling of water washing over my body when I dove into the lake or the feeling of a hug, but I would not lament those things.

I told myself, "Concentrate on what I can do." I repeated those words over and over in that hospital room and would continue to say them throughout my life. If I could succeed in not allowing thoughts of what I had lost to take over, I would find a way through this. It was the only way I knew forward: control what I let myself think. With nobody to guide me and no other way to manage the rest of my life, I clung to that. I was years away from the healing that would put me in the place to allow me to start Kids' Food Basket, an organization that first fed 125 elementary school children sack suppers and has grown to feed thousands of kids in my and other communities. But this was the beginning of it all: my drive to heal and to make my life meaningful, my love of life and belief that we are all connected and called to care for each other.

Over the course of the next few weeks in the hospital, every negative emotion from fear to sorrow to anger would haunt me, but each time, I would catch myself and fight my way back to thinking about something positive. Just looking around at the people in my hospital room and remembering that I had love helped. I would think about the future with Jeff and remember I had hope. There were still lots of things in life I could enjoy: picnics, movies, boat rides. A few years later, I had friends who even wanted to take me downhill skiing, convinced I could do anything. I told them, "Why would I go snow skiing now? I didn't even want to do that when I was able bodied." I could still laugh, and I could still make others laugh.

———

There were always doctors or nurses checking on me or family and friends stopping in to visit. I think the other patients must have wondered what was happening, how there could be laughter coming from one of those dreary rooms. My friends came to visit and after the initial awkwardness we would talk and laugh just like we always had. Eventually, everyone learned that to have a conversation with me, they would have to walk from one side of the room to the other as my bed rotated. Sometimes I would laugh at the strangeness, at how each visitor tried to time their movements to be at the right side of the bed at the right time, while seeming to be in regular conversation. If there is laughter, there is hope.

I was not supposed to have flowers in my hospital room because I was in intensive care. By June it was starting to feel like I was at home in the hospital, but I also missed the spring. I longed to see the grass unfurl in green sheets across the lawn, the flowers beginning to bloom, the sky the calming blue of springtime, with the sun brightly looking over it all. My family and friends knew how much I loved flowers and gardens. People would show up with just one rose each, just something they cut off their rose bushes. It felt like an act of rebellion, like I was still the girl who could do anything.

Marlene, who I had been living with when I met Jeff, came in to arrange the roses. As my bed flipped me toward her then away, I saw she had a row of medicine bottles.

"Where the hell did you get those?" I asked. She didn't

say, but I guessed it was from a nurse who was willing to break the rules. I'd turn one way, and she had 5 roses in various bottles. I'd flip the other way, and she was gone. Flip back and she had water dripping all over. As she put the roses in each medicine bottle, one would tip over. I'd flip back and see her trying to fix it, and then she would knock over another bottle. It was like dominoes, one bottle toppling over the next, splashing water everywhere. I burst out laughing at seeing her with the mess she made of the roses. She laughed with me, and it felt good.

I had to find humor wherever I could. There might have been tears behind the laughter, but we laughed anyway. When my family treated me just the way they always had, I knew that I would somehow be okay for real. But being okay wasn't a permanent state. There were times I would be okay for a while, and then without warning, a wave of fear and sorrow would wash over me. It took a long struggle to grasp the reality of my life and to come to terms with it.

When Mel came to visit me in the hospital, still bandaged herself, she knew I couldn't walk, but she couldn't understand what that meant.

"You still have legs," she said, peeking under the blanket at my legs.

"Yes, but they don't work anymore. Now they're just for sitting and I'll have a wheelchair to help me get places." It was hard enough to face it for myself, but so difficult to say out loud. Yet, Mel just nodded like it all made perfect sense to her. Seeing her acceptance helped me to accept a little more. Instead of walking, I would be riding in a wheelchair. Would it be that simple?

I tried to focus on the feeling of hope. But mostly I slept. It took so much energy to heal, and I needed rest. The mechanical whirring of my Rota-Rest bed as it flipped me from side to side often lulled me to sleep. There was a television attached to the end that rotated with me, so I could watch if I wanted. I welcomed the distraction, but it didn't stop my mind. As I flipped from side to side, my emotions flipped between grief and hope. Flip, and a sense of loss would overcome me. I could list a lifetime of things I would never experience, of possibilities lost, of dreams I wouldn't even dare to dream. I felt I had a right to feel that loss. I knew too well the temptation to settle there, in misery.

But I would not allow myself to do that.

Flip, and I would force myself to a new thought. After all the things that had been taken from me, I still had my family and my friends. I still had my selfhood, my mind, and my soul. However you define the self, I knew it went beyond physical existence. There was an essence inside me that would fight to come out, that would shout, "I'm still here." And in answer to that self, I felt I had no choice but to find a way forward. So, I struggled with those bad feelings, sometimes letting them get the best of me, but not for long. And over time, I grew stronger in my ability to fight back, to say, "I won't think about the things I cannot do. I will rejoice in what I can do."

Life Is a Process

Although the world is full of suffering, it is also full of the overcoming of it.

— *Helen Keller*

Before I could go home for good, the doctors were sending me to rehabilitation. I met with the team at a local rehab hospital, and they kept telling me about how great their program was. They had modeled it after a hospital in Denver called the Craig Hospital, which was world renowned for work with people with spinal cord injuries.

My cousin's wife was a nurse and she kept encouraging me to go to Craig Hospital for recovery instead. I was considering going to our local rehab, but I was diagnosed with a bladder infection, which delayed my transfer. While I had time to think, I made my decision.

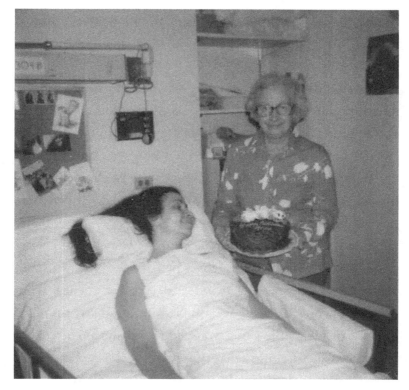

Mary K. with her mother, in the hospital.

"Damn, if they're that good, maybe I should go to Craig," I told my mom and Jeff. A part of me just wanted to go someplace else, to prove that I wouldn't be trapped forever. My sister Joanne came to the hospital and helped make calls and arrange insurance. The people at Craig were happy to take anyone from Michigan because our no-fault insurance meant payment for the best care. I felt lucky to be a beneficiary of the care our citizens and legislators decided was in the best interest of those who have suffered traumatic injuries. That legislation shows how much we value life, all life. I can't imagine how I would have managed without

Michigan Catastrophic Insurance. As laws change, I have a real fear for what will happen to others who suffer the same fate as me.

It was a difficult decision to go all the way to Denver for rehab because Jeff had to work, so he wouldn't be able to stay with me during my time there, and I didn't want to be away from him. I knew for my own longevity and the best understanding of my injuries, going would be the right thing for me to do. So, I went with my mom and with plans for Jeff to come the final week.

I had to be taken from the hospital that had been my home for three months to Denver by Air Med. It was a small plane, like a Cessna. I was wheeled in on a gurney, lying down, so I couldn't really see much around me. My mom sat in front of me, while I was strapped in, staring at the ceiling of the airplane. I could sense more than feel the plane lurch off the runway, climbing slowly until it reached cruising altitude, my ears popping. Then, even though I didn't have feeling in my body, I registered every blow of turbulence as the plane seemed to rocket through gusts of air. Fear washed over me, fear at how precarious the whole thing felt as I was rushed to a future I wasn't sure I was ready to face. I closed my eyes and prayed. I prayed for strength and courage. I prayed for hope. I prayed for Jeff and Mel, for my mother, and for my family.

I prayed the prayer of healing: "Loving Father, touch me now with Your healing hands, for I believe that Your will is for me to be well in mind, body, soul, and spirit. Cover me with the Most Precious Blood of Your Son, our Lord Jesus Christ, from the top of my head to the soles of my feet." I prayed the rosary, starting with the Apostles Creed, Our Father, and Hail Mary.

My mother joined me, "Hail Mary, full of grace, the Lord is with thee. Blessed art thou amongst women and blessed is the fruit of thy womb, Jesus. Holy Mary, mother of God, pray for us sinners, now and at the hour of our death. Amen." These were the prayers that I had learned to recite since childhood, and they became like a mantra, pulling my mind away from fear and sorrow. I didn't know then what I know now: prayer and meditation would become ways to occupy and strengthen my mind. That whatever my situation, the ability to breathe and recite a simple mantra, a single prayer, would infuse me with a sense of calmness and strength that would help me through fear, frustration, and even boredom.

Somehow, we made it to the landing and then the ambulance ride to Craig Hospital. During that time, I came to terms with a new realization. There is no such thing as control. We like to pretend we can control our lives, but that is just an illusion meant to protect us from the terrifying fact that most of what happens in the world, most of what happens to us, is out of our control. It took a long time for me to accept this, but once I did, it made living my life so much easier.

———

At Craig, I had a semi-private room where I lived for the next three months. I shared the room with a young woman from Texas named Mincy. She was very quiet and didn't like to talk, so I was left to use my time to work. And I worked every day, in a way I never knew was possible. The mental and physical effort I exerted during rehab was beyond anything I would have thought I was capable of. It was work in a way I hadn't considered because my very life depended on it.

Each morning, I woke up and ate breakfast with the help of hospital staff. My mom, who was living in family housing nearby, stayed with me all day. Breakfast was followed by Mat Class, which meant doing stretching and exercises for range of motion. This involved lying on a mat with the physical therapist manipulating my limbs, bending my legs at my knees or moving my arms around. I tried to help, tried to will myself to move, to use my mind to heal my body. But in the end, I just had to trust that while she made me move, my body was getting stronger, even if it was a strength I could not feel.

Next was lunch, then occupational therapy, where the therapist wanted to see what my limitations were and what I could do. I was given massages and the OT worked more on range of motion, which I began to understand was meant to keep my skin pliable and blood moving through my veins. I worked to keep my left shoulder strong to keep the ability I had to direct my left hand slightly with my shoulder movement. My right arm and hand had atrophied. As I lay there with the OT moving my limbs, I sunk deeper into the acceptance that life was not in my control. It made it easier to let her move me around when I couldn't move myself.

My occupational therapist was named Gail. I was 27, she was 24. Her mom was from Grand Rapids, Michigan, and she grew up in Battle Creek, Michigan. I also had a physical therapist from Detroit, who was around my age. It felt comforting to have people who could relate to where I came from and where I was now. Of course, I knew deep down that was absolutely untrue. No matter what their level of empathy or imagination, few people could understand what it felt like to be me, what mental and physical challenges I would face, what process I needed to go through to find a way to live a decent life. In my mind, I was still active, intelligent, capable. But my body would not cooperate. I tried to wiggle my toes, and the fact that no amount of willpower would allow me to direct this simple action in my own body was devastating.

As I worked at my rehabilitation, it became increasingly clear I was facing a lifetime of vulnerability, of reliance on others when I had only known independence before. If I let myself, I could wallow in an abyss of anguish. There were times when I felt so bereft, even with the other patients at Craig, who were going through the same struggles. Meeting and talking to them helped us all see we weren't alone. Acceptance was the best way I knew to mentally prepare myself for my future. I would have to accept help from others, and I was learning how to do that. Of course, I didn't know at the time how much help I would have; there was so much uncertainty. In the end, I learned having help was good fortune, and I would have more help than I expected, from attendants, from family, from friends. I was lucky in that sense, if luck could be invoked in a situation like this.

I was fitted for wheelchairs, electric and manual. That involved learning how to operate my wheelchair, how it would feel to be lifted in and out of it, how to ask for help. Is there a more difficult lesson to learn? I had always been good at getting people to do what I wanted. But that meant getting friends to go out and have fun or getting people to sign a petition that would benefit the community. Now asking for help would mean saying, "Will you do this for me, so I can survive?" Most of us would drown before asking for help. We have that American can-do attitude, that myth of self-made success.

I did not have that luxury. It was a vulnerable place to be, an incredibly humbling experience. But I had been brought up to believe that we are all connected, in families, in communities, in our humanity. It is our privilege as human beings to help and support each other. Of course, I had always thought of myself as a giver of help and support, which was much easier. Could I now accept help from others? I had no choice. The only choice I had was about the person I would be as I accepted aid from others.

Making lists in my mind helped me organize my thoughts and aided in memory, since I knew from now on, I wouldn't be able to write anything down. Just as I made a list in the hospital about how I was going to live, I made a list in rehab about how I would accept help. First, I would choose who would help me and I would have real human relationships with those people. Second, I would be grateful and show my gratitude. Third, I would be patient, realizing that no one could read my mind or do what I wanted as quickly or as precisely as I would do it.

———

Years later, I still see my main triumph during this time as the dominance of my temperament and attitude over my circumstances. Just like when I was in the hospital, I kept telling myself that even though I had no choice about my injury, I still had other choices. At this point, I couldn't stop myself from swinging back and forth between sorrow and hope, and my emotions were turbulent. I was, I repeated to myself, locked inside my mind, so I would continue to use my mind, and slowly gain the control I needed to face every day with some form of hope. I would fight against despair. It was as simple and as difficult as this: I would not let my mind settle into hopelessness.

I continued to practice what I started in my hospital bed. Every time I was in OT or having a meal fed to me and I had a burst of negative thoughts—and they would come often and when I was not anticipating them—I would stop myself and force my mind to think about what I wanted, what I had, what I could do. Over time, this became such a habit for me that I didn't even realize I was doing it. I would feel anger and grief for what I had lost, because let's be honest, this really sucks, and before I could sink into the feelings, my mind would take over and say, "Yes, but I have so many people who love me, whom I love. I still can think and if I can do that, I can do anything." I have no doubt that this habit saved my life.

So I went to occupational therapy, and said, "Thank you for your help, Gail," when it was done. For most people, occupational therapy is designed to help them regain independence in their lives. I knew that was not my goal. My goal was to determine what I would be able to do and to decide what I wanted to do. I could learn how to feed myself. If the table was at the right height and I had the right kind of brace, it was possible. But I would have to take hours for each meal, scooping food into my mouth in a way that felt messy and demeaning. I decided that accepting the help of my attendants to feed me was a better option.

My OT told me I could learn to write by holding a pen in my mouth and having the paper supported properly. "To what end?" I asked. I'm not a writer. Executives dictate their letters and documents, and others transcribe them. I could do that and accomplish so much more than I would if I struggled with the pen in my mouth. Hell, then I wouldn't be able to talk, and I much preferred talking.

Now, when I give Jeff a greeting card, I put on red lipstick and I kiss the card. That's my mark. My friends used to tell me, "You are the only person I know who can wear any color lipstick." I have 40 tubes of lipstick. Even Mel knew how much I love lipstick. Once when she was a teenager, she went to a garage sale. It was held by a Mary Kay distributor with extra stock, and Mel came back with some lipstick. She went into her room and tried the lipstick on, closed it up and walked out to where I was sitting. "Here, I got you this lipstick," she told me. I laughed and told Jeff, "I got a reject lipstick."

During my rehabilitation, I focused on getting as strong as I could in the ways that were possible for me. Of course, the biggest effort was still the mental adjustment, from being young, carefree, and independent, to NOT. But it was almost as awful trying to keep my shoulders, which I could move, as limber as possible and trying to get my body healed and to learn to deal with the constant tingling numbness. Anything that could improve my health, mentally and physically, from resting, to eating well, to using my time in therapy to come to terms with the future took all my energy. I prayed and meditated. Every afternoon, I went outside. After being confined to a hospital bed during May, June, and July, I didn't want to miss the summer in Denver, too, so my mom would push me along the garden paths or take me out to sit in the sun on the weekends. The mountains were visible from my window, and there was so much beauty. I felt the healing grace of God in that magnificent setting.

We also went on outings, the caregivers taking a bus load of us wheelchair users out to experience how it would be to navigate the world now. We went to restaurants for dinner and attended basketball games. The Craig staff put on a Halloween party. We went to the movies on Friday night with popcorn. They tried to make it as homey as they could to make the transition back into life seem possible. I was so glad that I went there. Everyone back home was worried about me, and I wanted to reassure them by making as much progress as possible. During the three months I spent at Craig, I thought, *Okay, we're getting somewhere. I'm still in a hospital but gaining on how to adapt to my life.*

After his accident actor Christopher Reeve said, "The longing for normalcy applies to every aspect of living with a disability, from health to relationships, work, travel and play." I wanted my normal life, but even when I recognized that as impossible, I wanted the life I lived to be as normal as I could make it. Until the 1970s when John Young got a

grant from the National Institute on Disability and Rehabilitation Research, there was almost no expectation that a
person with spinal cord injury would survive. That grant
was just ten years before I had my injury. Advances in all
fields of medicine fueled the idea that there could be a treatment, though not necessarily a cure. If the famous and
powerful like Lord Nelson, President Garfield, and General
Patton could not be saved after being paralyzed, then it was a
miracle that gave us the advances that have saved lives today.
I was grateful to be alive in a time when there was reason for
optimism. I was grateful to be alive at all. Knowing what
advances had been made gave me hope that there could be
even more done during my lifetime.

At the time I was at Craig, the doctors, and therefore I,
were always optimistic. There was a lot of research being
done and they thought perhaps during my lifetime there
might be a treatment, if not a cure. They were wrong. Today
doctors sometimes get people walking, but not after years of
paralysis and the atrophy that inevitably develops. There
have been gains in immediate care and now, instead of three
months of hospitalization and three months of rehab, people
with spinal cord injuries have just one month of each. They
work to improve strength. There has been talk of using elec-
trical stimulators or of stem cell treatment. I won't benefit
from those advancements when they happen, but I will be
thrilled to see them. I have remained cautiously optimistic
about robotics, but I can't help asking questions. What if I
was wearing a robot suit and it malfunctioned in the middle
of the street? I would be stranded. But then I remember that
any person's body can malfunction at any time. Most people

just live with the illusion that they are always safe, always in control. I just happen to have more awareness of the scary possibilities.

During rehab, I learned about all the complications I might experience as a result of my injury. I sat in the doctor's office in my wheelchair with my mom in the chair next to me. He was at his desk, which was neat and clear of any papers. *Doesn't he have any work to do?* I thought. I like order, but I've always got a lot of projects going on, so there are papers and other supplies all over my desk. But that was just a distraction from the serious list of complications he was telling us about. The list was long and unsettling. It included pressure sores, thrombosis, circulation disorders, autonomic dysreflexia, and the increased possibility of pneumonia and other respiratory complications, and depression, along with a bunch more.

"Who wouldn't be depressed after hearing that list?" I said to my mom. Then I laughed at my own sense of humor because what else could I do?

"Well, at least you won't get bored," she said. We laughed together. The doctor smiled. I don't think he was used to people finding humor in this situation. To me, the most important of these were the pressure sores and the respiratory complications. Pressure sores sound like such a minor thing, but if they get infected, they can result in a need for surgery or even in death. Imagine knowing that a tiny abrasion could have such consequences. I would learn how to prevent them if I could and how to deal with them if they couldn't be prevented. I told myself I had no choice. I had no choice.

I would be lying in bed or sitting in a wheelchair for the rest of my life, so prevention would be a challenge. There would be lots of opportunity to have constant pressure or friction to cause wounds. What's worse, I wouldn't feel them, so I might not know they were developing until it was too late. My caregivers would have to constantly reposition me so the same bones wouldn't be rubbing when I sat or lay down. They would have to inspect my skin to make sure sores had not developed. Oh, what a carefree life I had led up to this point, never having given such things a thought.

Breathing had already been a problem. At times, phlegm built up in my throat. When I coughed to loosen it, my chest seized up, like there was no way I could clear a passage for even the smallest trickle of oxygen to reach my lungs. It was terrifying. I felt like I was drowning even though I was surrounded by air. I would have to rely entirely on my care-givers to thump on my lungs, and when I got home, even Mel would learn that when she heard me coughing, she had to come immediately and apply pressure on my lungs to make sure I would keep breathing. It seemed like every minute of every day, I would be fighting a battle just to stay alive. Well, this life better damn well be worth it.

———

As I neared the last week of my stay at Craig, family and friends needed to be trained in my care. My mother's apartment was about a block away from the hospital, and I would be taken to stay with her once Jeff and Patty, an old friend who was going to be my primary care attendant, arrived. I had asked Patty to work with me because she was an old friend and she used to work at a nursing home, so I knew she had the skills. I wanted to be surrounded by people who I knew cared about me because I felt vulnerable.

Although I was expecting him, it was a surprise when Jeff showed up to the hospital in scrubs and walked around from room to room greeting people. I could hear the hospital staff talking. They were excited to have a new orderly, especially one so positive and upbeat. When he came into my room, he was laughing and talking with an actual orderly. He looked at me and said, "I guess it's time to start our new life."

"What are you doing in those scrubs?" I said, laughing at how silly he looked. Jeff did a little dance to show off his new clothes. He got more laughter and attention from the staff.

"You like them? I somehow ended up at the wrong hospital and borrowed these as a little joke." It felt good to laugh with him. It felt like happiness, love, and hope. As if we really would be starting our new life, just like we planned.

It wasn't going to be that easy, though. The doctors met with us to try to give us a sense of what life would be like. We sat in the conference room, with them on one side of the table and with my mom, Patty, Jeff, and me on the other. The doctors were trying to convince us that I should be put in assisted living for the rest of my life and that Jeff and I shouldn't get married. The doctors insisted that I would be better off without Jeff. They said statistics show that 85% of couples get divorced when one spouse has a spinal cord injury. Women were more likely to stay than men, they said, and we all knew Jeff was a man and therefore more likely to leave. If we went with probabilities, we would only last about a year to a year and a half, and then I would be worse off than if we had never been married. They said the best thing for me would be to make the best of my life while Jeff moved on. Everyone felt they were protecting me. Eventually they realized there was no stopping us.

"You don't know me," Jeff told them.

"You should know that life expectancy for people with your injury is about 14 to 16 years. You should make the most of your time," the doctor said to me. I couldn't answer because tears were welling up in the back of my throat and coursing down my face so that Jeff had to wipe them away.

"Why in the world would you tell someone in her position something like that?" Jeff asked for me.

"It's our job to prepare Mary K. for the life she has to face."

They might have been right, but at the time, it just felt cruel. I told myself, "Don't sit around and wait for things to happen." I laughed a little to myself; sitting around was exactly what I would be doing from now on. Jeff stood up.

"Mary K., don't you believe this," Jeff said to me. Then he turned to the doctors and said, "Can I ask you a question? Aren't all these statistics based on people living in assisted living and nursing homes?"

"You could be very right."

"Let me tell you something, Mary K. will be marrying me. She'll have her own house, her own garden, and the best care, 24 hours every day. When 1995 comes around, it will be just another year in our lives." He said that because, of course, we both had done the math and calculated that 1995 was the year they were predicting I wouldn't live past.

"We know what we're talking about," said the doctor. "Think about what you're planning to do."

"You think I'm going to be able to find someone else to fill her shoes? No way. It's going to be Mary K. and me 'til the end," Jeff said. I was glad he was doing the talking because I didn't feel like arguing.

That week in the apartment with my mom, Jeff, and Patty, I learned to trust in my caregivers, just as they learned to care for me. More clearly than at any point of my rehab, I was aware of my own absolute helplessness and complete dependency on them. These were people who loved me, whom I loved and trusted, but I was in every sense of the words putting my life in their hands. They would be my hands and legs, acting in the place of my own altered limbs, but even more than that, their care would preserve my life. I would soon learn that everything in my life was only possible because of the loving, dedicated attendants who acted for me, who treated me with patience and compassion, who believed that I should be able to live a life of activity and fulfillment.

———

Going home from Craig Hospital, I couldn't help but feel apprehensive. Having others do anything for me was totally unlike me. Now I would have to rely on everybody to do everything for me. I asked myself, "Can they actually take care of me? If I start coughing, am I going to choke? Will they be able to help me?" But by the end of the week, they learned what they needed to know.

Still to this day, I'm edgy about care, realizing how precarious my hold on life is, though never with Jeff because he has been with me so long, and he is a champion at it. Over the years, I have had a lot of different attendants, and many of them have been family or friends. Some can anticipate when I need a drink of water or need to be moved out of the sun, and some of them wait to be asked. Every time I receive an act of care, I am grateful. I may be more aware than most people, but it seems like every aspect of human life is smoothed over by the daily acts of others, and that is true for everyone, whether the stranger who helps carry the groceries to your car or the friend who calls when you're having a bad day or the partner who cooks a meal. And that's saying nothing about the life saving and life affirming actions of others.

It's difficult for many people to accept these acts graciously or to ask for them when needed. We have been raised in a culture of personal independence that makes being on the receiving end of help feel like a form of moral failing. My choice was to learn to rethink this attitude or to die alone without help. What if we humans recognized that we all need help sometimes? That many of the people who look like they are thriving by doing everything by themselves are often drowning when a life jacket is just within their reach? What if giving and accepting these acts of kindness, born of empathy, is what connects us all as human beings?

Just as nobody is above needing help, whether they are willing to ask or not, nobody is in a place where they have nothing to offer to help others. I can call a friend who is in a difficult place or provide a meal for a child in need of nourishing food, even if the hands that make the sandwich and pack the sack supper are not my own. Perhaps I needed to prove that to myself or to show it to the world. Perhaps I needed to be connected to our common humanity, not just by accepting care, but by giving care as well. Perhaps we all do.

Years after my stay at Craig, I reconnected with my occupational therapist, Gail, and she said, "Over the years very, very few patients have ever called me by name. They have just looked at me as a tool of rehab. You used my name." Hearing that made me feel pretty good that even in the midst of difficulty, I lived up to my own expectations.

When I remember those days, I think of all the friends I made at Craig Hospital, and afterwards, people who were injured in car accidents, skiing accidents, boating accidents, or even diving into a too shallow pool. There was Don, an insurance salesperson, and George who broke his neck when his car hit a horse. They all died within fifteen years. What kind of care did they receive? I can't really answer that, but I do know that survival in some sense all comes down to love: having people love you, loving others, and loving life.

In that sense, my life story is very much a love story.

DON'T SWEAT THE SMALL STUFF, BUT I AM THE SMALL STUFF

To every child—I dream of a world where you can laugh, dance, sing, learn, live in peace and be happy.

— MALALA YOUSAFZAI

My favorite picture of my mother Marion is one where she is sitting in a rocking chair in our living room, beer can in hand, leaning back. She always drank her beer from a can to save herself the work of washing another glass. With six kids, she had enough dishes to do. Next to her on the wall there's a hole in the plaster, big enough to be noticeable in the picture, so who knows how big it was in real life.

When I saw the photo, it was years later. I asked her, "Why is there a hole in the wall in this picture?"

My mom said simply, "I think one of your brothers threw another into the wall. That's where his head hit."

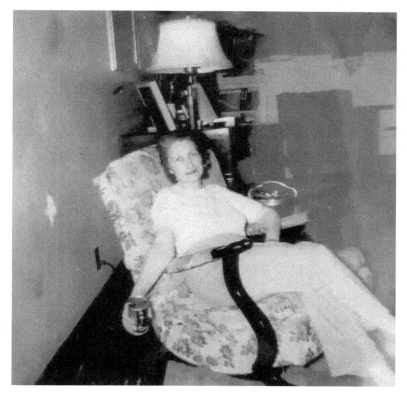

Mary K.'s mother, with a can of beer.

"Well, how about fixing the wall?"

"I'm sure we got around to it sometime."

That was my mom in a nutshell. She never worried or made a big deal out of anything. Every woman turns into her mother to some extent. When my girlfriends say, "You're turning into your mother," I say, "I certainly hope so. I hope I'm half the woman she was." My mom was the sweetest, smartest person I ever knew, someone who made everyone around her feel calm. She never gossiped or swore. I learned the art of editing what you are going to say from my mother, and that has been very valuable in my life. Not that I don't speak my mind, and anyone who knows me knows I swear all the time, but in any difficult situation, I put a bumper on what I am going to say, and doing so has been invaluable in bringing people to my side.

I had a girlfriend, Pam, who moved next door when I was ten years old. Pam would do an imitation of my mom, making her voice languid and low pitched. "Here's your mom: 'Gee, Tom, the house is burning down. I guess we'll have to get a new one.'" My mom is probably where I learned resilience. She lived by the philosophy that if today isn't good, tomorrow will probably be better. When people ask me how I have stayed positive and hopeful throughout my life, I always say that my parents and my childhood had a big influence on my outlook.

My mom was a lot like Harriet Nelson, the famous television mother on the show *The Adventures of Ozzie and Harriet*, and it's no surprise that the show ran during most of my childhood. Harriet Nelson had brains and talent and liked a good time, but she made the decision to be a wife and mother—albeit at a time when that was the main choice for women. Like the moms of that era, my mom wore red nail polish and lipstick, and she always wore an apron. She was always present and easy to talk to and spent a lot of time with her family, especially her two sisters and the boatload of kids in the extended family.

And with six kids in our immediate family, plus cousins, plus friends, our house could get quite chaotic. My sister Joanne was the oldest, and she always seemed above the fray, but following her were my brothers Tom, Dave, Mike, and Terry. Then me, the baby. The boys were always teasing and fighting. One time, Mike chased Terry around the house with a bat—at least it was hollow, Mike said—and got in trouble for his behavior. I can picture Terry responding, "Yeah, hollow like your head." Because a comment like Mike's couldn't pass without a little razzing.

My parents met when Mom was a secretary in downtown Grand Rapids after attending college for two years to become a stenographer/secretary. That's what smart women did in the 1930s. Every day she had to file papers at City Hall near Dad's law office, and they would often run into each other. They both came from big Irish Catholic families; my mom was the second oldest of five children, my dad the second youngest of eight. They both went to the same Catholic school, St. Alphonsus, though in different years. It just seemed to make sense that when they got married, they would have a large family, too.

I was born in October of 1952, the youngest of six children when my mom was 39 and my dad was 44. The five kids who came before me were all spaced out evenly two years apart. Then I came four years after my brother Terry. When I was older and figured that out, I asked my dad if I had been a mistake.

"If you would have been a boy, you would have been a mistake," he told me. After my sister, the four boys were a handful, and I don't think my mom would have survived another boy. My mom and dad went to the hospital for my birth on my brother Terry's fourth birthday. My parents thought it would be great if we had the same birthday, but the doctor said everyone needs their own birthday, so he delayed what he could and I was born at 12:25, just after midnight the day after Terry's birthday. I don't know if my parents were disappointed about the delay, but I do know that for years, my mom didn't want to make cakes two days in a row, so I always got the second half of Terry's birthday cake.

My dad, Tom, was bigger than life. He was 6'2", a big guy with big hands and a low voice, who loved to play practical jokes, loved to laugh, and loved sports. He played football in high school and earned a scholarship to the University of Michigan where he played tackle. He injured his back during play and lost his scholarship, so he transferred to the University of Notre Dame because he wanted to go to law school there with his two brothers who already attended. Hunk Anderson, who had taken over from Knute Rockne as coach of the football team for the Fighting Irish, sent my dad a note inviting him to watch their football practice. After that, he asked my dad to play, but Dad said he couldn't because of his back injury. Hunk sent him to a specialist who treated him and cleared him to play. After that he had a successful two years on the team and was totally dedicated to Notre Dame.

All my childhood, I never knew there was any other university than Notre Dame. My family members, and especially my dad, were their biggest fans. Dad got his law degree and returned to Grand Rapids where he practiced as an attorney and made a point about the importance of serving our community. He was the announcer at Catholic Central High School football games, and along with the work he did at our church, he was a member of the Elks Club and several other service clubs. Since Notre Dame didn't accept women when I started college, I went to Michigan State University. The year before I graduated, they started accepting women, and my dad asked me if I wanted to go. I did, but I was ready to graduate, so it didn't make sense to transfer at that point, but I'm still a fan of the Fighting Irish.

———

My childhood was typical for a middle-class white child of the 1950s and 1960s. My parents had bought a house after they got married in a neighborhood on the North side of Grand Rapids in Riverside Gardens. In 1939 that rambling Dutch colonial cost $7,000 cash. Even though that isn't a lot of money now, at the time it was a lot, and I can't imagine how my dad had so much cash. The Great Depression had been winding down, and war was winding up on the other side of the world. My parents already had one child.

The area was populated mostly by Dutch people who sent their kids to public school. Still, there were some Irish families like ours. All the houses on the street were pretty big, and plenty of kids lived in the neighborhood. I wanted to play with my brothers, but they would try to ditch me, saying, "You're too little. Go back home." I might follow them for a while, but they were faster, and I would be left behind. Even when I could play with them, I usually ended up in the worst role. I had to find everyone for hide and seek, or I was the monkey in Monkey in the Middle. They were faster and stronger, and they didn't let me forget it. As I got older, they weren't afraid to give me a pinch or a push, just like they did to each other, and when I got angry, I could dish it out just like one of the boys.

I spent a lot of time playing Barbie dolls and games with other girls in the neighborhood, and there were games of hide and seek with all the kids in the neighborhood after it was dark. As I got older, my friends and I played badminton and basketball and rode our bikes all over. There was a small creek nearby, Lamberton Creek, that began at Lamberton Lake and meandered over to the river. The kids from the neighborhood rode bikes to play at the creek. I loved that feeling of being off on an adventure with a group of friends, my legs pumping, the wind blowing through my hair.

No matter where I was out playing, dinner was at 5:30. We sat around the kitchen table and enjoyed the meal Mom made. She cooked goulash, Chinese food, and surprisingly good chili. Every Saturday night, we had hot dogs and beans. One time, my mom made meatloaf for dinner, which my brothers didn't like. They complained. Sweet as she was, my mother was not the greatest cook. She never said a word about it, but she also never made meatloaf again. The boys never even noticed. As we ate, there was always talk about what we did that day. My parents talked often about their volunteer activities. My mother was the Den Mother of the Cub Scouts. She was also a troop leader of Catholic Daughters, the guild at church. Along with all his other involvements, my dad was in charge of the Blessed Sacrament Parish picnic. Every year we collected money to buy sleds for orphan girls at Villa Maria on the West side. There was a focus on what it takes to be a participant in our community.

My dad had an extensive vocabulary with a lot of

obscure words and used them in our dinner table conversations. He would ask me what words meant and when I didn't know, I had to look them up in the giant dictionary on the bookshelf. He was also big on leadership, talking often about being a leader, and instilling in yourself what it takes to be a leader. As I got older, I could use this to my advantage because if he thought I was working on something important, he would let me do almost anything. We had an extension on our phone, and if I was on the phone too long, he would pick up the other end and listen in. When I heard the click of the line, I would immediately switch to talk about leadership—all of my girlfriends knew what I was doing, but I liked to believe that my dad didn't. After he put the phone back in the cradle, we could get on with our social plans. In real life, I was not so much of a leader, not in grade school or high school. In fact, I was not a very good student at Mount Mercy Girls Academy. I was lucky to have an excellent memory, so I just basically went to class, listened to what was said, and remembered it for tests. There wasn't much time for studying because I preferred to have fun.

My mother and father were very demonstrative of their love for each other. They would tell each other they loved one another in front of us, hold hands, and hug, but they never had fights in front of me. I have mixed feelings about that. If you grow up in a household where parents don't argue, you don't learn how complicated a marriage can be. You don't understand that even in loving marriages, there can be disagreement. My mother maintained they didn't want us to think anything between them was our fault. Later in life I told my mom that I thought she and dad did us a disservice by never arguing in front of us. I learned by watching them, and I never really learned how to fight in a marriage. She pointed out that I have never had difficulty getting people to do what I want without fighting—not since I had to negotiate my way into games and get attention from my brothers.

———

Our house only had three bedrooms, one for my parents, a dormitory style room for the four boys, and a girls' room. Because we were the only girls, I shared a room with my sister Joanne. But she was twelve years older, and I was really young most of the time she lived at home. I was eleven when she married and left. We had twin beds, and I would lay in my bed as she got ready in the mornings since she went out earlier than I did. The room would fill with the scent of the perfume she always sprayed before leaving, and I would yell and complain about it. I guess that didn't endear me to her, but she didn't want a little girl hanging around her anyway, and she always seemed so far away to me. She wasn't the type of sister to talk to a ten-year-old about makeup or boys or music. So, I was mainly in the company of the boys, if they would let me, or with friends from our block.

Since my mom was willing to live with a hole in the wall, you know she wasn't into decorating. Our house was functional and fun. We had a huge living room, and on Saturday nights, my mother would buy a six-pack of cans of pop, one can for each of us to drink as we hung out in the living room and watched television. Terry would lay on the carpet next to me, acting sweet, trying to get my pop—after being awful to me all week. Hoping to make his friendliness permanent, I would give him the last few sips. But it didn't work. The boys were wild and constantly teased and picked on me. I took it because I was little and because I knew that deep down this was how they showed their love for me. They would say it was all in fun and they were toughening me up. I was the baby of the family, but I couldn't be a baby to the rest of the world. My mother would tell me to just stay away from them. And I would answer, "They're everywhere. How can I stay away?"

As I got old enough to play games, the rule was that I got one game. That meant that if they were playing croquet or basketball, they had to put up with me until I lost, which was always too soon. It was tough being the smallest one all the time. But I'm sure as teenagers, my brothers weren't thrilled about having me play with them, and they probably thought of me as a little pest. Even though my brother Terry is closest to me in age, Mike, the next brother, was definitely the nicest to me. When Terry or the others terrorized me, my brother Mike felt bad. He actually made me my own little croquet mallet, perfect for a six-year-old, drew stripes on golf balls, and made wickets from wire hangers, so I had my own game.

The thing about my brothers was that although they teased me, I always knew they loved me and would help me if I really needed it. Along with my parents, they taught me to be resilient. I knew that every bad time was just temporary, and that it would go away and be replaced by a good time. A hole in the living room wall wasn't anything to get upset about. I never thought any trouble was permanent and insurmountable. Instead, I assumed I could find a way to turn it into a good thing if I just tried enough, was persuasive enough, and used enough charm.

————

Along with church, we went to Catholic schools, which also meant going to mass every day. In church I would sit in the family pew, and my brother Dave would sit at the very end so we younger kids couldn't sit with him. Terry would make me laugh during church. Mom wouldn't be happy. But I was so happy to be in on the fun. I embraced much of my Catholic upbringing and grew up to be an extremely spiritual person. Now, my relationship with God is very precious. It influences all of my decisions and interactions in life.

School was the important institution for me. It's how I got my name. My parents named me Mary Kathleen, but when I got to school, there were so many Marys: Mary Margaret, Mary Ann, Mary Elizabeth. To make myself stand out, I started going by Mary K. Of course, I couldn't go by Mary Kathleen, which was reserved for when my mom called me when I was in trouble.

Because our school building was small, every year the second and fourth graders were bussed for school to St. John's Orphanage, where they had extra classroom space. When I was getting ready to start second grade, my brother Terry told me horror stories about going to St. John's, as he had been through it twice and was now on to sixth grade. He said it was so scary, and the nuns there were mean. I was expecting to be haunted by ghosts and locked in a dungeon before I even got there. We had seen Dracula in a movie, and Terry said the school was just like entering his castle, dark and scary. It was an old looking building with peaks and spires and after Terry told me how awful it was, I cried and was afraid to go. But my mom wasn't going to put up with that, so on the first day of school, I was put on the bus and away we went.

In the end, the building was scarier than even Terry's wild imagination, and I looked up at the elaborate, gothic front entrance and had to force myself to walk in, talking and laughing with my friends. Once inside, it was just school. Sister Edward was my teacher, and I had all the same kids in my class, with the addition of one kid from the orphanage. Seeing kids without families made me think of all those trips we made each year to give gifts to the girls at Villa Maria who had been removed from their homes. I learned to appreciate all I had even more. It also helped me to see what my parents really meant when they talked about serving our community.

Even though I didn't love school, I was used to thinking of it as a place of safety, a place where everyone was concerned with me and my welfare. My family and neighborhood gave me the same sense. I can't imagine what it would be like if school were the only place that offered that sense of security. We as a country found out during the Covid pandemic that this was the case for many children, and that truth was heartbreaking. It was a call to action that I hope will not be ignored.

———

The best part of my year throughout my childhood was summer, especially because we spent summers at our family cottage from the time I was born until I was twelve. My mom's dad built it in 1921 and even though he died two years before I was born, my grandpa gave me the best gift of all, the place that held the happiest part of my life. After my grandpa's death, Grandma didn't want to go there as much, so my dad rented it from her every year. We would pack up our car and drive there the day after school ended and return home the day before school started again. Because my dad worked in the Waters Building in downtown Grand Rapids, which was only twelve miles away, he could drive to work each day from the cottage. As I got older, after my grandmother passed away, we had less and less access to the cottage as aunts and uncles and cousins took it over, though we always spent part of the summer there. In fact, I was there just the week before my accident.

It wasn't a big and fancy place. The cottage was small with three bedrooms, a kitchen, bathroom, and a big dining room with a table where we could all gather. We slept in roll-out beds on the screened-in porch on hot nights. The cottage was on a small incline, and my mom built a rock garden along the steps that led down to the beach. We had a large swing set, a dock, and a raft.

At the cottage, it wasn't just my immediate family. There were cousins and aunts and uncles who came to stay at various times. Having this extended family gave me a sense of belonging and security that helped me weather life's ups and downs. It also gave me an appreciation of fun and activity. We spent a lot of time swimming, and I learned how to water ski and sail. I remember going with my brothers out to the middle of the lake in a boat or to the raft my dad and uncles built twenty yards away from the dock, where we swam and played games like King of the Raft or Diving for Bottle Caps.

I was the type of kid who would go to neighbors' houses up and down the street and sit and talk to the mothers. I can remember talking to a lady whose husband started Frost-pack in Grand Rapids, now SYSCO, the restaurant supplier. We talked about makeup. At ten years old, I was not even allowed to wear makeup, but we discussed the prospect of my being able to wear it when I was 15. The neighbor lady across the street and I talked about gardening. Down the street a few houses, I would sit and chat with another neighbor. Her son was four years older than I am, my brother Terry's age, and they didn't have kids my age. I don't know what we talked about, but I would sit with her on the porch just passing the time of day. These women impressed me because they were nice to me, and I decided that I wanted to be that kind of person. Someone who was interested in other people. Someone who other people wanted to spend time with.

I grew up with a sense of freedom and expanding independence, which was one of the hardest things to lose in my twenties after my injuries. Every day of my childhood was spent in physically active outdoor play. Sometimes when I remember those little moments, it's hard not to slip into missing everything I have lost. There are a few things I especially miss, like canoeing; though I don't really miss ice skating or volleyball—probably because every time I played, I twisted my ankle. Those are things I probably never would have done after childhood, though not having a choice makes it harder. I would like to ride a bike again, to feel my legs pumping and the air whizzing past my face. When we go to a wedding, I would like to dance with my husband, but I have danced, and I know what dancing is like. I miss it, but I don't let myself dwell on it. I remind myself that I at least know what that feels like. I can imagine it, and then I shift my focus to the things that I can do.

I remember feeling that the world was open to adventure as my cousin Pat and I drove our motorboat across the lake at the cottage. We were eight or nine at the time, and the trust we were given was a big deal. It was exciting to control the machine as it dashed over the waves, and we saluted the other boats that passed us on our way to the far shore. There was a small convenience store on the opposite side of the lake, and our moms would give us change to buy candy. Pat and I would plop our coins on the glass counter and hear them ring throughout the store. Then began the process of picking: what did we like best, what did we have enough money to buy? Would he share his Good N Plenty if I shared my Lemonheads? We would return to the boat, pockets bulging with treats, and make our way back home, another adventure on the horizon.

One Fourth of July, when all the family was at the cottage, including our grandmother, we decided that the fireworks show put on by the lake association would not be enough. We wanted our own fireworks show. Terry was about seventeen, and at thirteen, I was thrilled to be his assistant. The big problem was that Grandma was afraid of fireworks. Even during the show over the lake, she would stand in the cottage in fear for her life, believing that the cottage would burn down. It's amazing that we went ahead with the show because our grandmother seemed so unhappy, but I attributed that to her being a widow at a young age. She stood tall like a statue and rarely smiled, even on a good day. Nevertheless, she loved her family and was there for the giant party we had each year with all the aunts and uncles and cousins, over 100 people, with food and drinks and even a keg of beer, which I would help ice down the night before.

We had been lighting off fireworks all summer, but this day was going to be even better. We drove pipes into the ground on the beach. The plan was that we would shoot a firecracker in the pipe, and it would propel a can into the air. We also strapped Roman Candles onto the swing set so they would shoot out over the lake. The fireworks went great, but the Roman Candles started shooting over the lake, then up, then up toward the cottage. Terry and I looked at each other. Grandma was up there. One hundred people caught onto what was happening at the same time. They all turned in unison and ran for the cottage. When we got there, we saw terror in her face.

I don't even remember what kind of trouble we got in, but I do know it was bad. Still, I loved that feeling of exhilaration when the fireworks started. There's something about putting a plan you made into motion, even against all logic and circumstances, that is absolutely electrifying. All my life,

I have loved to come up with a plan and then mobilize people and resources to make it happen. And even if everything doesn't go the way I thought, it can still be fun and worthwhile. You can still learn from the experience. For instance, this time, I learned: Don't make Grandma mad.

———

My parents had gone to the World's Fair in New York City in 1939 for their honeymoon. When I was eleven, it was held in New York again, so my parents decided to take me, Mike, and Terry. The theme of the 1964 fair was "Peace through Understanding." There had been conflicts in Asia after the end of the Korean War, with tensions high in Vietnam, but President Johnson hadn't sent American troops yet, and in our corner of Michigan, war and peace were not issues we focused on. There was civil unrest in the country, but the race riots in Detroit, on the other side of our state, hadn't happened yet, either. And we didn't see much of that in Grand Rapids, not because racism didn't exist, but because it was hidden behind what appeared to be niceness. Still, the World's Fair was a learning experience for me, and it's one of my first memories of seeing the kind of diversity that I never encountered in my small world of neighborhood, school, and church.

Of course, there was New York City itself. Skyscrapers blocked the sky on some streets, and people rushed from building to building with purpose. The cars on the road were dense, weaving through lanes, honking horns, making dangerous turns. I thought, *How do these people drive here?*

There certainly wasn't a place to ride a bike or even to walk without getting jostled, as five million people had flocked to the city for the fair. There were noises and smells I couldn't have imagined before, and everything felt so exciting. We went to Central Park and to various restaurants. We took a ferry to see the Statue of Liberty and toured the Empire State Building. It was a time when, whatever the reality, I truly believed America was the land of the free and anyone who came here would be able to build a better life. I still like to believe that, but now I've seen how different the lives of children can be through my work at Kids' Food Basket and other nonprofit organizations. Many of the children who receive sack suppers are from families of migrant farm workers. Our food supply in the United States is dependent on their hard work, yet they don't earn enough to buy food for their own families.

But at the time the Fair was exciting. What would the world be like in 2064? The GM Futurama building was full of innovations. There was a car that looked like a little spaceship, but there was also a Lunar Rover that would float easily over the moon's terrain. There was an atomic powered submarine for exploring Antarctica, and Aquacopters that looked like dinosaurs that could dive all the way to the ocean floor. In the ATT display, there were working Picturephones. One person could call from NYC to Chicago or Washington D.C., and they could see each other on a small screen. You both had to go to a special terminal, and it cost $16 for three minutes. That would be like $150 today. I didn't have anybody to call, but it was wonderful to imagine what might be possible in my lifetime. The whole fair was dominated by the Unisphere, a giant steel sculpture of the world with three rings around it that stood for the three satellites the United States had circling the globe.

And then there were the people. In my school in Grand Rapids, everybody was pretty much the same: white, middle class, and churchgoing. I didn't see much diversity. At the Fair there were 80 restaurants with food and people from different countries, along with all the people who had come from different parts of the country and different parts of the world. The instance that stands out to me the most is when we took a taxi back to our hotel. Our taxi driver was a Black man, and as we were driving, a group of Black people walked in front of the cab. I remember thinking they must be friends and I wondered why the taxi driver didn't wave to them. I had such limited experience and knew so few people of color that I just assumed they all knew each other. Even though that assumption was innocuous, it still reflects my basic ignorance about race. These ideas intrigued me, and I started a lifelong interest in gaining understanding of different cultures. I have always thought that if you have a different color skin or different culture and ethnicity from me, I'm very interested in what makes you tick and where you come from. I think people who are different are more interesting than I am because they know something I don't.

I ended up feeling the way I felt whenever I visited a new place. Certainly any time you experience a new city, even if you visit in a book or on television, it helps you understand there is a big world with lots of different cultures and lots of ways to approach life. You become more aware of the nature of the community that you live in and the importance of community. The place you grow up in and the place you live have a bigger effect on your life than you think. I decided I liked where I lived because it was a happy medium: enough people around to make life interesting, but not so many that there was no space.

Don't Think
Too Hard

*Parents can only give good advice or put them on the right
paths, but the final forming of a person's character lies in
their own hands.*

— *ANNE FRANK*

High school was totally different from grade
school. If you asked me if I liked going to
Mount Mercy Academy, I would have said no.
But I didn't hate it either because my friends were there. I
liked to talk and goof around more than I liked to pay attention and learn. Going to a Catholic school with its strict
rules and high expectations wasn't really my idea of fun. But
there was never a thought of anything different. Everyone in
my family attended Catholic schools. We all attended Blessed
Sacrament for grade school and my brothers went to
Catholic Central High School.

Tom and Marion Roach, 1938.

My sister Joanne and I went to Mount Mercy because when she was in eighth grade, my dad was at the drugstore and while waiting in line he talked to two girls who were really nice. This made my dad think nice girls went to Mount Mercy; I don't know what he thought about the girls at other schools. By the time I got there, Joanne was married, having graduated in 1958. Other girls in my class came from big families like mine, so they had sisters that old, too, which was just one of the many things we shared. The girls at Mount Mercy came from schools all over the area but most of us were Catholic. We all came from similar backgrounds and had the same kind of home life. At least that is what I assumed at the time. Of course, it's impossible to know what really happens in a family if it's not yours. It was an era when if you had struggles or problems, you put on a good face to go out into the world. We Mount Mercy students were aware that our family did the extra it took to afford to send us there, so we tried not to complain.

Except about the uniforms. We had terrible uniforms: brown loafers, brown knee-high socks, brown skirt, brown vest—at least the blouse wasn't brown, but it was plain white. In the late '60s when miniskirts and bright colors were in style, we really stood out. If I had to wear those clothes, I would at least walk with confidence and make sure I looked as good as possible. I read in a magazine about Carnation's Slender and the Sexy Pineapple Diet and tried to follow them. I didn't think pineapples could be sexy, but apparently eating them could be.

At the end of the school day, a bunch of us girls would meet in the restroom. We would take off our vests, tie up the tails of our shirts and hike up those loose slouchy skirts to make ourselves look better. Then we would put on make-up, giving each other tips and sharing lipstick colors. I loved gliding lipstick onto my lips and then making a little pucker and kiss toward the mirror. It was a great send-off, this sign that we were ready to go. Then we girls would get onto the city bus and go downtown to sit in coffee shops to sip Tab and talk to boys.

I, of course, felt like I needed to live up to my parents' expectations for me. So, I volunteered at a senior living center to help with meals. I had read what Jacqueline Kennedy said about her husband after his death: "John Kennedy believed so strongly that one's aim should not just be the most comfortable life possible, but that we should all do something to right the wrongs we see, and not just complain about them. We owe that to our country, and our country will suffer if we don't serve her. He believed that one man can make a difference—and that every man should try."

Living up to those high expectations didn't mean I couldn't have fun. There were so many ways to have fun and so many ways to get into trouble. In school, we used to tease each other by pushing someone's head down when they were drinking from the drinking fountain. Maria and I did that to a friend one day, and she turned around to chase us. We ran laughing and shrieking through the hallway, forgetting where we were. She chased, we laughed and ran faster. Until Sister Arlene Mary, our principal, heard us. She stepped into the hallway just in time to stop Maria and me. That meant a trip to the principal's office. Sad to say, it wasn't my first and it wouldn't be my last. The bad part was that my dad was sick at the time, so as we sat in the front office waiting to be called in to meet with Sister Arlene Mary, I started to worry that my parents would be called, and I knew how they would feel. My mom would worry, and my dad would be disappointed. It was too late to go back to change what I had done—that was a lesson I learned early in life. Followed soon by "No regrets." Either don't regret what you have done or don't do things you know you will regret later.

But that day, I was still young. Tears welled up in my eyes.

"You're so good at turning on the waterworks when you need to," Maria said.

I have to admit, a few tears at the right time had saved me a lot of trouble, so I had gotten pretty good at making them happen. I didn't tell her that they were real this time. I just said, "What if they call my parents?" She patted my hand and we waited for our sentence. We were suspended for a couple of days, and I had to take the bus home to tell my parents myself.

Another time, my friend Maria and I decided to skip school and go straight to the coffee shop. As the other kids gathered in front of school and marched toward the gothic arches at the front entrance, we slipped away and rushed to the bus stop. We hopped on the downtown bus and rushed to the back, giggling with excitement. Were we really doing this? There is something so frightening and thrilling about breaking the rules. I imagined Sister Gretchen in first hour, calling roll and noticing I wasn't there. Would she call my parents? I squashed that thought down right away. We were already on the bus, so there was no going back. Just another instance in my life when I would realize that there was no way to turn back time and undo what I was doing.

We didn't have time to fix ourselves up beforehand, but when we got to the coffee shop, we ducked into the bathroom before anyone could see us. A few adjustments, and I felt presentable enough to be seen in public—a public not made up of my fellow classmates. I put on some Revlon Red lipstick because it was dangerous and rebellious, and I blew a little kiss toward Maria. She smiled and said, "You look good in any color lipstick. You're so lucky."

"You look good, too," I said. We laughed and went out to order coffees. We sat at the cafe table right in front. I was pretty sure nobody I knew would be walking by to catch us, and we looked good, so I wanted to sit where we could see and be seen. Maria and I talked about our classes and some boys we liked over our coffees, but soon our cups were empty. We hadn't planned ahead very much, so we didn't have any place else to go and it was still morning. We spent the whole day realizing what a dumb thing we had done, until it was time to go home. So, we felt a lot of excitement, but then nothing happened, which was a letdown. That's just the way some adventures go.

———

I had already decided it was better to have fun than to be good. There were so many ways to have fun, and maybe get into trouble, when I was young. There were high school dances at Catholic Central. In summer we hung around with a bunch of people who went to public school. And there was an ice cream shop where we hung around, laughing and talking until we got reprimanded.

When my older brothers were in high school, my mother said to me once, "I wonder what the boys think I would do if they shared the details of their lives." I guess she suspected they were out doing things she didn't know about. But I assumed that because she said so to me, she expected totally different behavior from me. I know that if I thought my mom and dad might say no to a request, I would do what I wanted and hope they didn't find out. I learned that lesson when my brother Dave asked to go to a dance being held at the Black and Silver Room at the Civic Auditorium. My mom asked, "Are there going to be public people there?" I guess she was worried that if he hung out with public school kids he would get into trouble. I have no idea where she got that idea, but it showed me that I would be better off asking for forgiveness than permission, as the saying goes.

Once my friends and I were old enough, driving gave us even more freedom. As one of the younger students in my class, I got my license later than my friends. I was surprised when my parents let me ride with friends, but they didn't seem concerned. Of course, I never told about the time I ended up in a joy ride in a car that turned out to have been "borrowed" without permission, but that felt like a rite of passage, so many kids did it.

And then when I got my driver's license, I couldn't believe what a joy it was just to hop in a car and go where I wanted. Of course, I didn't have my own car, but my parents would let me use theirs if I was going someplace. I could drive to meet friends or to go to football games at Catholic Central. And there were always boys. Most of them would rather drive than be driven around by a girl, but if a group of us planned to meet somewhere, I always wanted to be the one to drive.

Driving gives you a sense of freedom and control, so I don't fault boys for wanting that, but with Women's Liberation, I was starting to see that girls could have the same thing. My dad had raised me to be a leader, so it felt natural to be the one who was in charge of the transportation.

I would get together a group of friends and drive us out to the beach at Lake Michigan. I loved basking in the sunshine and diving into the cool, clear water. When it got too cold for that, I would try to find other adventures. One time I drove a carload of friends out to a small town outside of Grand Rapids, and we went exploring in the cemetery there. We walked through the headstones, looking at the names and dates from the past. When we were done, we headed home, but I couldn't remember the way back. We didn't even know the name of the town we were in. We drove around for a while and then finally it got so late, I stopped at a gas station to get directions home and we made it without incident. It's ironic that being in a car is what took everything away from me, yet I still associate driving with freedom. I still miss being able to hop behind the wheel and go where I want, without hassle or waiting on other people.

When we were seniors, the schools had a new program called Community Education. People could take classes like interior decorating, psychology, anthropology, and other subjects they couldn't teach in high school that would give us a leg up in college. At Mount Mercy, we attended regular school in the mornings then juniors and seniors could go to Community Ed. This was a great opportunity to learn a lot of new things, but, of course, it was also a chance for more fun. I met my first serious boyfriend in psych class in Community Ed. After classes, we used to drive to open land and park with another couple, where we would drink

Ripple, a cheap red wine. Amazingly, that land now belongs to Kids' Food Basket. I jokingly told our farmer at the new urban farm that story and he told me, "If I ever find any Ripple bottles buried here, I'll make a shrine to you."

Now, looking back, I am so glad that I made the time to enjoy life and to experience as much as I did. I wasn't born with a disability, so I know what it feels like to swim in the Great Lakes or run through a field. When you're young you have no idea what the future will hold, what forces beyond your control will push into your life. Living a life of joy and fun with people you care about in the present is the best way to insure against a future that may not turn out as expected.

―――――

When I say that the consistency of my parents' presence throughout my childhood gave me the strength to get through everything I faced in life, it is with an awareness that not all kids are as lucky, no matter how much their parents love them. Now I realize what a luxury this was, and if I could give everyone a gift, it would be to have a foundation of care and support in childhood. I knew my parents would always be home for dinner and that I could rely on them for their kindness and care. When my older siblings were growing up, my dad was still working hard to establish his practice with his brother and another lawyer, so he wasn't around as much for them, but my mother was always in the kitchen. In that sense, I grew up in a different home than my older siblings, especially Joanne, who must have seen me as this baby girl demanding attention that my dad hadn't had time to give her.

No matter what, we never lacked for anything. I do remember that we only had one car, as was the case for most families at the time. My mom would drive my dad to work on the days she needed the car to do errands. One time we picked him up from work, my mom driving, and Terry and I in the back seat. I was asking my dad for this and that, all things a girl needs. I didn't have any understanding of family finances, probably because it wasn't something we worried about. My dad turned around to me and said, "Sure, and while you're asking for things, can you ask your mom to sew another patch on my sweater?" I was used to the way he teased me, even if the comment went over my head at the time. I knew that if I needed anything, I would get it. Eventually I would learn the important lesson that getting some things might mean that I would have to give up others.

All of this is to say that even though I describe my childhood as idyllic, it wasn't without the normal family fracas. There's a possibility I am remembering it as better than it was as compensation for all I've lost. Remembering itself is painful because I wasn't able to continue my life on the path that was set in those early years. It's easy to idealize my childhood, and it was wonderful, but it means that my loss was even more devastating. But most of us who dream of being ballerinas or doctors follow different paths as adults. And there are kids who live without those dreams because they are just barely surviving. My parents were typical of their time in offering their children every opportunity, though it was nothing like what parents do today.

I'm aware that it was a different time. Between World War II and the 1970s, we had increasing prosperity, and while there were definitely disparities, all Americans were benefiting from economic growth and advances in technology. There was a general sense of hope. We also didn't have access to as much news and social media, so we weren't aware of the differences that existed between our way of life in the suburbs and others in urban and rural America. We had a sense of duty towards others, but we also had a sense of our place in the world. I never saw real suffering or poverty. And I definitely never thought about the systems that kept people in their places.

Today we have even more awareness of the disparity between kids who have and kids who don't, of those who suffer from neglect and abuse, of those who live with food insecurity, even in loving homes. We can all work to change this. As author and activist Glennon Doyle says, "What if we decided that successful parenting includes working to make sure that all kids have enough, not just that the particular kids assigned to us have everything? What if we used our mothering love less like a laser, burning holes into the children assigned to us, and more like the sun, making sure all kids are warm?" Looking at the world this way certainly would change how we use our resources.

I was shielded, and my first real trauma was the accident that caused my injuries. Up until then, my ideas about other people's suffering were abstract. My ideas about how I could ease that suffering were practical and limited, shaped by my parents' belief in service to our community and being prepared to lead. If someone was sick, find medicine; if someone was hungry, give them food. In a way this helped me to be more effective when I started Kids' Food Basket. It meant that I could focus on just the practical need to feed kids who needed nourishing food. We packed a sandwich, a drink, and healthy snacks in those sack suppers, and that felt like an accomplishment. The job of looking at the way the world works and changing systems came later.

CHERISH YOUR
RELATIONSHIPS

Part of the problem with the word "disabilities" is that it immediately suggests an inability to see or hear or walk or do other things that many of us take for granted. But what of people who can't feel? Or talk about their feelings? Or manage their feelings in constructive ways? What of people who aren't able to form close and strong relationships? And people who cannot find fulfillment in their lives, or those who have lost hope, who live in disappointment and bitterness and find in life no joy, no love? These, it seems to me, are the real disabilities.

— *FRED ROGERS*

W hen I was graduating from high school, I asked my mom, "What should I do now?"

"You need to be with people your age, so you should go to college," she said in her simple, straightforward way. Problem mentioned, problem solved. That was the way my mom taught me to deal with life. Basically, the expectation in my family was that you would at least try college. Grandma Roach, my dad's mom, went to college in Georgia in the late 1800s, when very few women attended school after twelfth grade. She was the big push behind my dad and his brothers going to college. The local junior college had a program that interested me.

So, I started at Grand Rapids Junior College for an associate degree in Early Childhood Development. Just like in high school, I listened during classes, but I struggled. I didn't study and I didn't really understand professors' expectations. But, as in high school, I used my memory and could usually pass any test simply by repeating back what I remembered the professor had said during class. That kept me going the first years. The second part of my program had a component where we could attend Michigan State University.

When I found out I was going to be living on campus at MSU, I realized I needed to find people to live with. Cindy Williams, a girl I had met at Mount Mercy, was in the same program. I saw everybody in the Commons at GRJC and thought maybe she would be fun to live with, so even though we hadn't really hung around together, I asked her if she wanted to live together. She said yes, and she knew another girl, Debbie, from Junior Achievement, who also had a friend who needed someone to live with, so she made our fourth.

Cindy Williams, left, and Mary K. Hoodhood.

During summer semester, we lived on campus and attended classes. We experienced an odd combination of a sense of freedom and finally being at a big college campus at the same time the campus was pretty much closed down and felt almost like a ghost town. When I walked along the sun dappled sidewalks between the impressive buildings, I imagined the whole place was mine.

We lived in the medical student dorms at the edge of campus, and our space had been converted into a two-bedroom apartment. There was only one other person living on the fifth floor with us, and the hallways echoed with our laughter as we walked together to and from classes. The building felt so vast and empty that we rode our bikes up and down the long hallway. Since it was summer and the cafeteria was closed, we had to make our own meals. I had actually started GRJC in Home Economics, so I took over the cooking. I always loved cooking, finding recipes, planning menus, going to the grocery store to pick out the ingredients, and then standing in the kitchen, immersed in the cutting and measuring and frying. The smells and textures of the foods made me feel alive, almost as alive as rushing to Meijer grocery store in Debbie's red Mustang to buy the food. There were times when I felt like I was traveling to another world as I made spaghetti or sweet and sour chicken. In a way, making food was a way to have another adventure, a way of visiting another culture.

Because we lived in a medical building, behind us was what seemed like a huge garage, but we soon found out it was actually where they brought in cadavers for medical students to learn from. We could look out our fifth-floor window and see ambulances come in with the cadavers. We had a class called Fishing and Wildlife, which required binoculars. As the bodies were rolled into the operating room, we watched from our window with our binoculars. It added to the eeriness of living on an empty campus.

That was the only thing our Fishing and Wildlife class was good for, as far as I was concerned. It fulfilled our science requirement and fit into our schedules, so we all took it together. Most of the time, we weren't in a classroom. The class was in the evening, so sometimes we went out to look for constellations. We went out into fields and woods and roped off an area to study then logged the kinds of bugs and plants we found there. Bugs weren't really interesting to me, though I did okay on the tests because of my memory. Everyone laughed at me because one time when the question was about the constellation Orion, I wrote "O'Ryan."

"That's the Irish spelling," I told the professor when he asked what I was thinking. He didn't see it as funny. I wanted to tell him that he needed a sense of humor. Just about anything in life can be funny if you have the right attitude.

We also had to take a field trip on a bus to northern Michigan for Fishing and Wildlife class. I made bologna and PB and J sandwiches for us all that morning, so getting ready and getting to the meeting place took longer than I expected. We were the last ones to get on the bus. When we got there, our professor was standing outside the waiting bus with a clipboard and a very unhappy look on his face. I wasn't super happy, either. Any outing that required work boots and bug spray wasn't really for me. Plus, we kept stopping in different places, getting off the bus to look at patches of grass or woods and then getting back on. I was tired from the night before and decided I had had enough.

After multiples stops along the way, I wasn't getting off one more time. My friends sat with me. The other students trudged off the bus, but I could see most of them weren't happy either. Finally, one said to the professor, "They're not getting off. Does that mean we don't have to if we don't want to?"

"That's fine. If they don't want to participate now, they

can do it when they have to retake this class in order to pass." So, we got off. It was a required class, after all. When I finally graduated, one of my friends said to me, "The only reason you graduated was because you just kept signing up for college classes." I had to agree. Let's just say I took advantage of the social aspect of college.

———

The campus filled up again in the fall, and we were still there, though we needed to move to another building. I looked through the student newspaper and found a sublet. Four nursing students who lived in Twickingham Apartments were gone Sunday through Thursday because they had clinicals in Detroit. That meant only three days when they actually used the apartment. They had an extra room and were looking for one person to rent it. Deb, Cindy, and I went to meet them, since our fourth roommate was moving in with other friends. She felt her grades were suffering from hanging around with us. At first, I could see the nurses thought we were crazy, but I convinced them that we would all be out a lot, and it would save everyone money. It was only for a semester, and then the rest of our program was back in Grand Rapids, so we didn't want a full year lease. They agreed. The four nurses shared one room, and the three of us shared the other. There wasn't going to be a lot of privacy, but it would be fun.

The apartment was far from campus, so it was a long walk to classes. That wasn't a problem, though, because I figured I could always hitchhike. When I planned my schedule, I always assumed I could hitch a ride, so I only had to leave a half hour early for classes instead of an hour. The way I saw it, if I had a car on campus, I would be happy to give a ride to anyone who needed it, so I assumed anyone who stopped would feel the same way. It was a great way to meet people, too. Hitchhiking only got me in trouble one time.

I was alone in the apartment when the phone rang, so I answered it.

"Is Linda there?" said a voice on the other end of the line. A nice sounding voice, I thought.

"Sorry, wrong number," I said. Something made me add, "Why do you want to talk to Linda anyway?" He answered, and pretty soon we were having an hour-long conversation.

"Look, I have to go," I said. "Call me again sometime."

"I don't know what number I actually dialed," he said, "just the number I was trying to dial." We both laughed and I told him my number. After that, he called, and we talked several times. Finally he asked to meet, and we set up a meeting at Berkey Hall for the next week. Why not? He seemed like an interesting guy on the phone. In the meantime, he sent me a dozen roses. I couldn't decide if it was romantic or a little overzealous. But what happened on our next phone called put me squarely in the overzealous camp.

"I think I know who you are," he said. This was the first time he sounded creepy instead of flirty.

"How do you know?" I asked.

"I've been doing a little investigating," he said. "We'll see if I'm right tomorrow." After we hung up, I started thinking about this guy I had seen lurking around sometimes when I was on campus. Could it be him? I went into our room and talked to Cindy.

"You know that guy I've been talking to? We're supposed to meet tomorrow."

"That's great," she said.

"That's what I thought, but now I'm not sure. I think I know who it is, and he's a little creepy. I've seen a guy around on campus, and I think it might be him."

"Don't go then."

"If I don't go, I'll never know for sure who it is. Plus, I think he knows who I am," I said. She agreed to come with me, and we hitchhiked to campus the next day.

When we got there, the guy who I was worried about was standing outside Berkey. I didn't know what to do. I went over and talked to him for a second, but then said it was nice meeting him, but I had to go. As we were walking along with our thumbs out, a car slid to the side of the road. We ran up and jumped it.

It was the guy.

He didn't even ask where we lived. He just drove straight to our apartment. Cindy had gotten in the front seat, and I was in the back. We tried to keep up a casual conversation until he got to our apartment, and then I jumped out as fast as I could. Cindy followed and we rushed into our apartment, hearts beating like crazy. When we closed the door behind us, I didn't know whether to laugh or cry. I didn't have a chance to find out. There was a knock at the door. I looked at Cindy and she looked at me with wide, scared eyes.

"Get rid of him," I mouthed, and I ran into the bedroom. I could hear him asking for me.

"She's not available. Whenever we get back from campus, she jumps right in the shower," I heard Cindy say. Of course, the shower wasn't running, but he didn't know that. Somehow, he accepted defeat and went away.

That's when I befriended a fraternity. At the time, fraternities and sororities were not a big thing. In fact, in the era of anti-establishment sentiments, most of us stayed away from the Greek system. But the guys we met were cool, and they called us their sister sorority. We got the "official" name of the Crazy Sisters. The drinking age had changed temporarily to 18 when I turned 19, and that was my sendoff to college, so I was ready for a party. Why not? When I had papers due, I knew somehow they would get done. While everyone else was running around being nervous about grades and anxious about the work they had to do, I said, like my mother did before me, *things will work out. If today doesn't go so well, tomorrow will be better.*

And there was time to have lots of fun. My brother Terry's in-laws had a concession stand at the football games. Terry worked there, and after the games, we stopped by the stand, and he would give us bags of leftover popcorn. They were long plastic bags, almost as tall as me, and I would lead everyone home from the stadium like the pied piper offering handfuls of popcorn as my temptation.

Our fraternity friends invited us to a Homecoming Dance. All the girls were worried because nobody had brought a nice dress to campus. "Don't worry, I'll call Terry and he can grab a bunch of dresses from my closet back home and bring them when he comes to sell popcorn on Saturday," I told them. We were supposed to be having fun, not worrying about every little thing. Most things have a solution if you just take a second to think. My dad had taught me to be a leader, and I was leading my friends towards fun. Gathering people you cared about seemed to be the most important thing you could do with your life if you asked me. So that's what I did, found friends and learned about their lives, found fun things for us to do, and supported them when they needed it.

Because we all need help and support from time to time; not everyone has it easy all the time. One time Cindy came to me almost in tears. "I just found out I have a paper due before Thanksgiving break. I thought it was due after the holiday. I don't think I can get it done in time. I'm going to fail." She looked like she was going to cry or break out in hives.

"What class is it in? What are you supposed to be writing about?" I asked. She told me and I knew right away I had a solution. "My dad has a book all about that. I'll ask Terry to bring it to us, and you can use it to write your paper. It won't take any time at all." Problem presented, problem solved, just like my mother.

"You always have my back, Mary K. I know I don't have to worry about things getting taken care of when you're around," Cindy said. That made me feel good. That's what a leader does: makes people feel confident about doing what they have to do. My dad was right.

I had been studying to be a teacher, but once I got into a classroom of 25 seven-year-old kids for my student teaching, I realized it wasn't for me. Kids are loud and they ask a lot of questions. They demand so much and run around with boundless energy. By the end of each day, I had a headache. There are plenty of bad teachers, and I didn't want to be one. There are so many dedicated, excellent teachers, and I thought I should leave the students to them. Social work seemed more in my line. I had a clear understanding that there were people in the world who didn't have what I had, and in the tradition of my family's commitment to service and leadership, I wanted to help people. Everybody kept telling me there was no money in being a social worker, as though teaching might just be the path to being a millionaire. I knew I wasn't going to be rich and that didn't bother me. I wanted a life that was meaningful, a life where I would connect with other people and make a difference.

———

I graduated from Michigan State in 1973. Right after college, I worked as a lobbyist for the Association of Independent Colleges and Universities of Michigan (AICUM), a public information association for Aquinas, Albion, Adrian, and Sienna Heights, among others. It was a good job for me because I never had any problem asking people for what I needed, and usually they would give it to me. I never really thought about that as a special skill when I was younger, but I soon realized that it wasn't something that most people felt comfortable doing or succeeded at. I liked the freedom of living on my own, close enough to my family to see them when I wanted, but far enough away to be living my own life. There was so much in the world to experience and so many people to meet. I didn't want to miss a thing. I stayed in Lansing to work. *This is the life*, I thought. I had a job I enjoyed, a great apartment, friends to have fun with, and a cool car—a 1970 silver Mustang with pinkish interior.

Then I got a phone call from my brother Terry. "Dad had another stroke. He's in the hospital." I barely took the time to hang up before I packed a bag and rushed home. He had had a stroke several years early and had recovered many of his abilities, even continuing to practice law part-time. This time at 68, when he was sent home from the hospital, he could no longer practice as an attorney. I traveled back and forth between my job in Lansing and my family in Grand Rapids. It was difficult to see my vibrant bear-of-a-man father dwindle. My dad died in 1977. I was alone with him and my mother in the hospital room. At the time, I thought, *What is my mom going to do?* That was when I really learned how strong a woman my mother was. I expected her to fall apart, but she had that Irish Catholic mentality that said we are here on earth to prepare ourselves for the next world. She carried on preparing for the next level without him with the same quiet strength she had shown when my dad was alive.

I was twenty-five when I moved back to Grand Rapids, and I spent the next couple of months working and seeing my family and friends. In March of 1979, I was working for my sister and brother-in-law. I also got a job going door-to-door surveying people about the city directory. It was enjoyable but sometimes tiring work. By the time I was twenty-six, I felt like I had a clear sense of direction. I rented a room from my friend Marlene, had fun going out whenever I wanted, and still saw my mom and family regularly. My sister

Joanne would often come over to visit and we would sit around and give ourselves manicures and catch up on life.

My girlfriend Shelley worked as a bartender at Snug Harbor Bar. It was a chilly night, windy, and I felt like I needed to get out, so I went to have a drink with her. I never had a problem going out by myself; in fact, I preferred it because I could come and go as I pleased. Finding someone I knew wherever I went in town was pretty easy. When I got to the bar, I saw my former roommate Cindy's brother with friends and sat with them. Later, I went to the other side of the bar where I saw some guys I knew playing pool with a new guy who was cleaning up the table. Intrigued, I watched for a while. Another guy I knew from high school was sitting at the table next to me with a couple of girls I knew from Catholic Central.

I leaned over and said to one of the girls, "That guy's cute, but he's too young for me."

"He's our age," she said, "but he's really a hood."

"What?" I asked. He didn't look like a hoodlum. He looked like a bouncer.

"His last name is Hoodhood." I thought that was a funny name, and wondered why I had never met him before, since we knew some of the same people. Then again, he clearly wasn't Irish Catholic with his dark complexion and black hair. I stayed and watched him play pool for a while, but eventually got bored, so I decided to leave. As I was walking toward the door, one of the guys I knew waved me over.

"Where are you going?" he asked.

"Nothing's happening. I'm going home."

"Wait a minute. I want you to meet my friend. Mary K. Roach, this is Jeff Hoodhood."

We were standing by an empty table when Jeff came over to talk, so we ended up sitting by ourselves, and my friends seemed to disappear from my notice. I was focused on Jeff, thinking, "He talks a lot, but he's funny and smart." I laughed at his jokes and felt like we really hit it off. He said he worked at a jewelry store and installed car stereos on the side. Industrious, my dad would have liked that.

"Quarter's up," someone came over to say. Jeff had left his quarter in line on the top rail of the pool table to mark his turn.

"Want to watch me play?" he asked. I went over to the pool table. I already knew that he was a good player from what I had seen earlier, but he kept scratching.

"You're pretty good, but you missed some easy shots. I guess I make you nervous."

He laughed and didn't seem to mind, and when the game was over, he asked me, "Want to get a drink?"

We ordered drinks, and Jeff excused himself, clearly to go to the restroom, though he didn't say so. The waitress came while he was gone, so I paid for the drinks. When he came back, he was a little miffed and said, "I would have taken care of that."

"I'm sorry, pal, you're just a little slow on the draw tonight." I took a sip of my sloe gin fizz. Jeff was drinking orange juice because he was in training for a weightlifting tournament. I was interested in him, so I decided to get straight to the point. "So, what's your deal? Tell me about yourself."

"I'm shy," Jeff said, with a sly smile that invited me to contradict him.

"Yeah, you're shy alright. You're shy like a boa constrictor."

"I'm a weightlifter and I have a huge tournament in Chicago in two weeks. It's the Windy City Open," he said. I could tell he was excited about it. I loved anyone who was passionate about life. "I would be honored if you would come with us."

"Are you going to win it for me?"

"I'm going to try." Then he hit me with another sly smile. "Ask your mother if you can get away for the weekend."

"Stop right there. I'm 26 and I don't have to ask my mother. Stop trying to see how easy I am." We both laughed at that. We talked for a long time. I could tell he felt the same way I did: like we were just in sync, like we had the same mindset. I didn't want the night to end, and I could tell Jeff was trying to linger as long as he could, but eventually we had to leave.

As we got up from the table, he asked, "Where do you live?"

"Down Burton."

"I live a few miles away, by Breton Village, so we live close together. I'd be honored to take you home. You're safe with me."

"You idiot, how do you think I got here? I drove my own car."

"I'm going to follow you home just to make sure you're safe." And I felt safe with him, knew instinctively he was someone I could count on and trust. But I didn't spend all those years growing up with four brothers to let a guy off easy.

"We'll see," I said. We got outside, and it was snowing, typical Michigan in March. Jeff had a big jacket, but I always wore layers with a sweater because I liked to be prepared for anything, and it was too much of a hassle to carry around a coat. We lingered at our cars talking, not wanting to leave. I shivered a little in the cold, and Jeff opened up his jacket so he could wrap it around me. I felt my heart leap.

"Can I kiss you?" he asked.

"Okay," I said.

He kissed me and said, "I knew it would be like that." So did I.

He followed me as I drove home and came to the screened-in front porch at Marlene's house. We stood out there talking and we kissed again.

"Well, I'm going to bed, and you're going home." I didn't say what I usually said when a man walked me home, "I don't even know you. You're crazy, I'm not sleeping with you." He seemed to know we had something worth waiting for.

"I'll call you," he said. And I knew he would. But when he had driven away, I realized that I hadn't given him my number.

———

The next day, he called me at work. I told him I was going to Lansing with a girlfriend for a few days.

"How about we go out Friday?" He invited me to his parents' house where I met his brother, mom, and dad. After they went to bed, we went into his bedroom. I thought this was a good way to get to know him. On his nightstand was a picture of him doing a bench press with a little girl on the end of the bench.

"Who is that little girl?"

"Who does she look like?"

"You have a daughter," I said thinking this was his way of sharing something important with me. "She looks familiar. Where does she live?"

"Her name is Melisa. She lives with her mother and stepdad in town." It took me a while to realize who she was. Her stepdad's cousin married my best friend from high school. I had actually met Mel at the wedding with her mom and stepdad. It just felt like another way Jeff and I were connected. I stayed and we talked until I thought it was time to leave. As soon as I said I was going, he had his jacket and hat on.

"Where are you going?"

"I'm going with you."

"No, you're not," I said. He laughed. Everything we said to each other felt original and witty. I liked that he thought I was funny and that he was funny, too. We saw each other every day after that and went to the Windy City Open over the weekend. We had the time of our lives. Jeff placed high in the tournament.

He asked me to marry him two weeks later.

"We'll see," I said. "But I believe in long engagements." Here's the thing about Jeff: he is so off and so unique and so crazy that he's entertaining to me. I get his sense of humor. He had the right work ethic, the right family ethic. I knew when I was with him that I'd have more fun than being by myself. With other guys, I felt like I could have had more fun by myself. He was a different type of guy than I usually dated. My answer might have been yes if he had had a ring.

We continued to date over the next few months. Jeff was still working at the jewelry store, but he was building up his car stereo installation business, too. I was impressed at how he balanced both, but also made sure that when it was his weekend with Melisa, he was totally present for her. I met Melisa officially and loved her from the first time I saw her. I loved her for herself, but also because she was part of Jeff.

A lawyer we knew invited us to a Christmas party. I realized that I hadn't seen Jeff dance. "Do you like to dance?" I asked.

"Of course," he said. And then he quoted me one of his favorite movie lines, "'We had one dance, one short dance, which meant everything, and it lasted a lifetime.'" I wasn't sure what movie it was from, but I liked the quote. It showed how just a little bit of joy could sustain you for a lifetime. Of course, I wanted a lot of joy—there was so much to experience in the world. But I would start with one dance. The party was being held in the old Seidman mansion on Reeds Lake in a ballroom on the fourth floor.

I wore a black velvet skirt with a silver top. When I arrived at his parents' house, Jeff said, "You look more beautiful than ever." I could tell by the look in his eyes that he really thought so. The thrill of warmth rushed to my face, and I blushed. Before we left for the party, Mel came downstairs from where she was waiting in Jeff's room. Jeff gave me an engagement ring, and Jeff and Mel said, together, "Will you marry us?" This time, I knew it was for real.

"Yes, of course." That was all I needed to say, and we were off to celebrate in a rush of excitement and love. At the party, we got to see people we knew and tell them our good news. It felt like the perfect start to our beautiful life.

I had agreed to rent the room in Marlene's house for a year and the lease was just about up. Soon, Jeff and I moved into an apartment together. We settled into a wonderful time. Most Sunday nights we would be at the Green Apple Bar on Alpine and 4 Mile Road. Jeff played pool. I'd watch and talk to people. We also spent a lot of time at the beach at Lake Michigan or at local lakes. Jeff's brother bought a jet ski, and Jeff got one, too, so we could go together on Green Lake or Lake Macatawa. We brought Mel whenever we could.

She was just five years old, going on six, and Jeff had had limited visitation since his divorce, every other weekend from noon on Saturday until six p.m. on Sunday. Mel was very quiet and a sweetheart. I knew she already had a mother, and I was in no way trying to take that space, but I wanted to be part of her life. I noticed she couldn't read, which my nephew and my cousin's daughter could already do. So, I went and got some books and games and taught Mel how to read. Love of reading has always been part of a close bond for us.

The way we combined our two lives felt so natural. We shared everything from the important to the trivial, from my love of cooking to Jeff's love of cars. I enjoyed tooling around in Jeff's 1973 Super Beetle. It was such a fun car. One time when I was driving, I thought the engine sounded loud, so I took it back to Jeff.

"What did you hit?" he asked.

"Nothing, come see for yourself."

We drove around and he could hear that it was the muffler. Jeff always had a toolbox in the trunk, so we pulled over into the loading dock at my sister and brother-in-law's building to change the muffler. When we finished, my hands were black, and I laughed and reached out for him. Jeff didn't flinch. He leaned in and kissed me.

"Look at that. There's nothing we can't do together," he said. And I felt the same way. I had never had any trouble being on my own. I enjoyed my own company, and when I wanted, could always find someone to have some fun with. But with Jeff, the whole world felt different, like I could relax and sink in, like there wasn't anything that could daunt us.

BUILDING A NEW DREAM

You may not always have a comfortable life and you will not always be able to solve all of the world's problems at once, but don't ever underestimate the importance you can have because history has shown us that courage can be contagious and hope can take on a life of its own.

— MICHELLE OBAMA

The good news was that after my rehabilitation I was able to go home from Craig Hospital on a commercial flight with Jeff pushing my wheelchair and lifting me into the airplane seat beside him and my mother, across from Patty. It was a bit of normalcy that I needed to start the next phase of my life. Like my mother always said, "*Mañana*, we'll be good tomorrow."

My time at Craig Hospital helped me solidify a lot of my ideas about how I was going to live my life. I learned how to deal with my physical challenges and started to build my plans for dealing with life mentally and emotionally. That doesn't mean it was the final version of me. Like anyone who moves from their twenties into their thirties, and eventually to their seventies, I would change and grow as a person. I would experience ups and downs, not just regarding my paralysis, but from living a life full of activities and connections with other people. I may have had to be more self-aware because of the need to be mindful of my thoughts and emotions, but I still wanted to live a life like everyone else.

Melisa helping Mary K. with makeup at the campground.

I'm well aware that some people who see me feel sympathetic, know immediately that no matter their circumstances, their life is easier than mine. Their thoughts show in their eyes. But mostly I know that they are wrong. I have been happy even though it has been tough. My life is definitely worth living, and it has been filled with purpose, joy, and love. I find things to laugh about all the time. But I want to make sure that people don't discount me or others who are not in the mainstream of society. I have always believed in the value of life, but after my accident, I was even more committed to building a life that would exemplify this.

On the other hand, it's a big burden we place on people who are different, expecting them to be inspirational, to overcome every obstacle, to make us all feel good about our humanity. I don't want my life to be one more brick used to wall people with disabilities into a tiny room of expectations and limits. I want to live my life for myself, for my family, and for the good I can do because I am me, not because I have a spinal cord injury, not because I use a wheelchair. I want my friends and people who know me to like and be interested in me *for me*, just the way I am interested in them and their lives.

———

When Jeff and I got home, we had to navigate enormous difficulties. We found a first-floor apartment with a ramp and an accessible bathroom, but Jeff was determined to save up to buy a house. That meant that, like so many brides, I had wedding planning and house hunting to keep me busy. Unlike so many brides, I had to manage this along with dealing with insurance, accessibility issues, and finding competent care.

Because Joanne had been such a bulldog when dealing with the insurance companies, I had full-time attendants when I got home. Patty was with me from eight a.m. to five p.m. every day, then a new attendant, Kevin, a neighbor from my childhood, would arrive from five p.m. to nine p.m. My mom came to stay with me pretty much every day, even when I had an attendant. She wrote letters for me with her beautiful handwriting. She paid bills and did small tasks and some gardening—things I had done for myself since I left for college but could no longer do.

Overnight and weekends, when my mom had other obligations, it was just me and Jeff until I saw that wasn't going to work out and we were able to hire more attendants. Saturdays were his busiest time because most customers needed weekend service for installing car stereos. That meant I would sit in my chair alone all day, and he would come in to check on me as often as possible. I spent a lot of time watching TV, which I admit is what I would have done anyway. Basically, he was working twelve-hour days, six days a week, plus taking care of me on weekends and nights. And during this time, I rested, sat in my chair, hired and learned to manage attendants, practiced patience, prayed, and planned our wedding.

Of course, I already had my fantasy wedding planned; I had been thinking about it since I was a little girl. I didn't let myself be distracted by others' expectations and just focused on making myself and Jeff happy. Still, I wanted to have the wedding as soon as possible because I knew my mom wasn't entirely pleased about my living with Jeff before marriage. She never said anything, and I'm sure she realized it was best for me, but I knew she would be happier if we were married. So would I be. I had returned home from the hospital in

November of 1980 and our wedding was set for August 1981.

The first big issue was the church. I had three cousins who were priests, and the oldest would conduct the ceremony, but that didn't make it easier to navigate the Catholic church. There were the Pre-Cana classes required for all couples, designed to help the man and woman prepare for the sacrament of marriage. Every church in town held them in a little classroom in the basement, and there was no way for me to attend. Kindly, my priest at St. Alphonsus waived this requirement.

Next, we had to deal with Jeff's divorce. At the time, my church didn't recognize divorce, so Jeff wouldn't be allowed to remarry. Annulment was our only alternative. Then we found out that the Church also didn't recognize Jeff's wedding because he was Antioch Orthodox married in a Christian Reformed church. Unfortunately, neither church would allow a priest from the other to bless our marriage or perform part of the ceremony in their church.

"Haven't these people heard of the ecumenical movement?" I asked Jeff. Apparently not, so we had to make a decision. Jeff said he would be fine if we went to my church, especially since I wanted my cousin to perform the ceremony.

We also had to deal with our family members, who had been convinced by the doctors at Craig that marrying Jeff would only do me harm in the long run. Jeff and I had no doubts that he would stick it out, and I knew we were the ones who mattered. I was right, and after over 40 years of marriage, I want to go back to those doctors and say, "Na na na na na na!" My friends knew I was doing the right thing and they were all supportive, so that helped.

Of course, I wondered if my disability was going to be too much in addition to the fact that it isn't easy to be married anyway. I wouldn't be an intelligent human being if I didn't think seriously about the choices I was making. But part of me thought only so many bad things can happen to one person. I deserved this. I deserved love and security, and happily ever after. The truth is that not everybody gets that —in fact, a lot of people don't. But when Jeff and I talked, I felt such certainty. We were so in sync with each other, our humor, our values, our goals in life. We were so in love. Certainly that would serve us well. Whatever was happening on my exterior, inside I was still the same person. I would not lose myself because of physical limitations. Life was ahead of me, and I intended to embrace it, to find happiness, to create a purposeful existence. And I knew Jeff would be with me.

———

As I adjusted to life in my wheelchair, I created a guest list, chose invitations, chose the venue, food, cake, and decorations. Buying a wedding gown was a challenge. After so many months in the hospital, my body had changed, and it was difficult to try on dresses. We found a beautiful white dress at a bridal shop in Grand Rapids. It was designed as a bridesmaid dress, so it was simpler than a formal wedding gown with all its layers and puffiness. My mother was able to alter it so it fit me perfectly. I found white ballerina shoes to go with it. My niece Stephanie, who was 13, would be my bridesmaid, and she helped me with my hair and makeup because she loved to do that. Melisa was the flower girl. Jeff had his brothers stand up with him.

The day of our wedding arrived, and I was both excited and sad. I had planned every detail for a beautiful day, but there was no escaping the sense of grief at what I had lost. My father would not walk me down the aisle. I would not carry a bouquet. I would not dance at my wedding. "Stop this," I told myself. Dwelling on what I didn't have wouldn't change anything. It definitely wouldn't bring me happiness. Instead I made a list of what I did have: a man who loved me and stood by me through everything, a daughter who I loved, a beautiful church full of family and friends who loved us, a meaningful ceremony that would set the course of my life in many ways, a big party to look forward to as a celebration of it all, a future that was open to possibilities. There is always hope.

When I planned the day, I knew I didn't want to be wheeled down the aisle. The priest who would be performing the ceremony, my cousin, Father Bob Bek, helped me come up with an alternative. Before anyone arrived, I was ready. My brothers helped me sit in the Presider's Chair in the chancel of the church in front of the altar. They turned the chair facing away from the congregation. The chair was like a huge wooden throne, and nobody could see me sitting there. The guests weren't visible to me as they filtered into the sanctuary. I heard the footsteps and the murmurs and the swishing of people sliding into the pews while I sat there. I prayed for myself, for our marriage, for

Mel and the big part of my life she had become. The organist began to play, first quiet background music and then the bridal march. I waited.

My brothers came over and each stood at a corner of the chair. Slowly they lifted me and turned me to the sanctuary. This felt like their blessing. It was just like in childhood when they would tease me, but in the end show their love and support. I thanked them quietly and then focused on the pews ahead of me. I couldn't believe it. The nave was full, as though this were a holiday mass. Of course, we had invited 400 people, but I didn't realize what that would be like until I saw them all gathered there in one place, a community of support and love for this next phase of my life. My mom was right in front, and Stephanie and Mel stood close by, looking lovely. Awed gratitude washed over me.

I looked up at Jeff and could see he felt the same way. There was love in his eyes when he looked at me, and I hoped he could see the same thing in my eyes, through the welling tears that I blinked back.

"You look beautiful," he whispered to me. I wished I could take his hand in that moment, but I would have to convey everything with my eyes.

My cousin stood between Jeff and me in his robes and his stole. "England is not the only place they are having a royal wedding," Father Bob said. Just the month before, Princess Diana had married Prince Charles. I bet nobody told them they wouldn't make it—life is so unpredictable. Everyone laughed at Father Bob's quip—many were his cousins, so he had a receptive audience. The ceremony went by and even a few moments later I barely remembered it.

This was my first reason to celebrate in a long time, so we planned a huge reception. It had been difficult to find a place that was big enough, so we held it at the Grand Valley Armory Hall. It wasn't the most beautiful venue, but it would fit everyone. We had a live band. Our friends catered the food, and we hired a bartender. Jeff was concerned about paying for all the booze for my family—it's hard to get away from those Irish stereotypes—and in this case, I have to admit my family drinks a lot. "I'm concerned about paying for all the food for your bodybuilder friends," I countered.

The cake was the centerpiece of the room because it was so big and glorious. One of my cousins was married to the nephew of Arnie from Arnie's Bakery, probably the biggest and best bakery in town. As a gift they offered any cake I wanted. It was the most incredible wedding cake you ever saw. Before we cut the cake, one of my cousins sang, then Jeff's aunt sang. They had beautiful voices. Everyone was eating, drinking, laughing, and having a good time.

At one point, my brother Mike leaned over to kiss me and dumped his whole beer on my lap. "I can't believe you did that," I said. He rushed to wipe it up, apologizing, the same kind boy I had always loved. "Oh, well," I said, "I always like smelling like beer instead of perfume."

I had decided against a formal first dance. I'm not shy but I didn't want to be the center of attention in a wheelchair. It was for the same reason I didn't want to go down the aisle. I was still trying to get used to the idea of not walking, of what that would mean for me and for all of the parts of my life. If I was able bodied Jeff and I would have had a first dance as a couple. There was a sense of loss, but I minimized it in my mind. Then my new father-in-law grabbed my wheelchair and pulled me around the dance floor. We were rolling around to the music, the closest I would get to dancing, and it felt exhilarating. Unfortunately, he slipped on some spilled beer and fell, so we ended up just sitting there, me in my chair, him on the floor, laughing. A friend said to me, "You're like a clay pigeon. You can't get out of the way." Even now, at parties if I get stuck talking to people, I can't walk away.

We followed the tradition of throwing the garter and bouquet, though Stephanie threw the bouquet for me. All in all, it was a wonderful but exhausting night.

We went home to our apartment, loaded with gifts and good wishes. We had decided against a honeymoon because it felt like too much. There would be a time for us to travel together, but this wasn't it. I lay in bed feeling the exhilaration of the night and hopes for the future. My next task would be finding us a house. Jeff said the only thing he cared about was a garage, one that was big enough for him to build up his business installing car stereos.

———

I started my first week of marriage thinking about the kind of home I wanted, the kind of home I needed. Besides the garage for Jeff, I knew I wanted a garden. I needed to see the crocuses peeping through the last remnants of winter snow and the tulips that would mark the spring. I had missed one entire spring in the hospital. I wouldn't miss another. I would have flowers blooming throughout summer. A deck would be nice, too. Our home would need to be open enough for me to maneuver through with my wheelchair. And it would have to be a place where our friends and family would gather. I had already learned one of the most frustrating parts of my situation: I couldn't just hop in a car and go out to visit friends. I couldn't drive, of course, but no one we knew had a house that was accessible for me. People would have to come to me, so I would have to have a home that would welcome them.

It's so easy to become distant from others in times of trouble. In the midst of difficulties, reaching out can feel like burdening others with our problems. But even before that, we have to recognize when we are in trouble and be able to say it to ourselves, which, of course, is almost impossible for a lot of people.

When trauma first hits, friends and family come to offer support and casseroles. Over time, though, as a person lives with grief over the loss of a loved one, or chronic illness, or the results of injuries that will not heal, it is easy to slip into awkwardness. What is there to say? There's no way to fix things, no flowers or donations to a cause that can make anything really better. People have their own lives to deal with, and it can be trying to visit a friend who has been suffering for a long time. The reasons are varied and nuanced but they all come down to one thing; whether we are in the position of facing challenges or as a concerned onlooker, we often define people by the situations they find themselves in. We say *my friend who is a widow, my friend with cancer, my friend who is paralyzed.* And it takes real effort to go beyond that to the shared humanity that is the foundation of any relationship.

I couldn't just walk over to the neighbors' houses to talk about makeup or gardening, as I did when I was an adventurous kid, and I couldn't drive over to visit friends to tell them about the amazing thing Mel did the last time we were together or what a nice evening Jeff and I had or to ask them about their kids or how their parents were doing. But when we were together, I would make sure that I met any person on a human level. I've always found others' lives interesting. I still wanted to hear about my friends and family members and what they were up to. My interests include history, home decor, cooking, volunteering, the latest book I've read, or a news report that made me think. I want to share all that and more. I am not a one-dimensional person defined entirely by my disability. Even though I was tired a lot, I would save up my energy to invite friends over for dinner or coffee, or some project I was working on. It took effort on all sides, and I can see why it is tempting to drift apart, but I will never regret that I put my energy into people or into creating a home to welcome them.

I got a realtor and started looking, having either my attendants or Jeff, when he had time, drive me to the houses we found. Finally, I found the perfect one. It had belonged to a Grand Rapids police detective, and he had built an extra garage to refurbish trucks, which would be just what Jeff needed. For me, there were over four acres with lots of area for a garden.

Renovations to make the house livable for me took three

months. My insurance company put $50,000 into the house before I could move in. At the bottom of the basement stairs, before they were made accessible, there was a platform, with two steps to the right to enter the family room, and two steps to the left to enter the laundry room. There was no way for me to get into the basement. In Michigan, where tornado watches send us fleeing to the basement for safety, this was an issue. But even more, for me, it seemed wrong that I couldn't get to a part of my own home. When so much is taken from you, sometimes a little thing is one thing too many. We were able to have renovations done to install a lift. I can roll onto it, and someone can push a button so it will take me to the basement. We wanted to make the house more accessible with sliding doors, which are easier for a wheelchair to negotiate. Insurance would pay for a slider for the deck off the bedroom, but not on the other side. It was an extra $800. I said, "I'll pay because I want to be able to go out."

We also had to build ramps along the sides of the house so I could get in. We made the bathroom shower accessible. Next to the shower was a dressing room which we ripped out through the closet to make room for a bathroom wide enough for wheelchair access. We had to raise the garage door to accommodate a wheelchair van. Almost all of the doorways had to be widened to get through in a wheelchair. I was so grateful for the insurance money that covered the costs of building ramps and widening doorways. Today I would have had to pay for it all myself. Now there's a financial cap on how much insurance will cover. Most people have no clue what it costs to live if disabled, not to mention medical bills. Without the insurance benefits, it would have been almost impossible for me to live a near-normal life with a home and family. No person should be denied that opportunity, especially since it is one of the ways to increase life expectancy.

I was so excited, repeating to myself, "Wow, we get to live in a house." I had spent so much time in the hospital, rehab, and a small apartment. In a way it felt like a luxury to have all of the renovations I needed. Really, I would have preferred to live a life that didn't need accommodations and accessibility.

Just like many buyers, I had buyer's remorse when we first moved in. I didn't know how we were going to live when I wasn't able to work, and it was difficult to imagine paying for everything at that point. I would wake up in the middle of the night crying. When Jeff heard me and asked what was wrong, I'd say, "What were we thinking? Do we have enough money to live here?"

"Don't worry," he'd say. "We're going to be okay." Those were the same words I would say to him when he woke up from another nightmare about the accident. It was a miracle we ever got any sleep.

FAMILY IS THE MOST IMPORTANT THING

Having somewhere to go is home, having someone to love is family, having both is a blessing.

— *IRISH PROVERB*

Once we settled into the house, it was time to settle into the reality of daily living. Excitement, adrenaline, and sheer willpower had kept me going so far, but now I thought to myself, *I'm a married woman. I don't have to do anything. I can watch TV and eat bonbons if I want.* The truth is that I felt lethargic, low energy. If I did something during the day, I needed a nap in the afternoon. If I got up and went out, after a couple hours I had to lie down until the next day. I remembered the days of my childhood and young adulthood when I could run all day—biking, canoeing, sailing, skiing. Now it took as much energy as I had just to open my eyes in the morning.

The Roach family.

Emotionally, I felt like I was handling what had been given to me from the trauma of the accident as well as could be expected. I was getting used to my attendants, Patty and Kevin. And, of course, my mom stopped by all the time. I felt nurtured by Jeff and his care for me.

I needed time to adjust physically, though. It was amazing to me that without the physical activity of running around all day working and doing things, I still felt so exhausted. I was only in my twenties. It took me quite a while before I felt like I could go out for hours at a time. I spent a lot of time lying around, taking naps, and letting my body heal. Surprisingly, the mental understanding of what was going on felt easier than the physical part. I just didn't feel right. I had to get used to not being able to control my body, along with the physical sensation of being paralyzed. While my body tingled like it was sleeping, I didn't have a true sense of where my arms were or if my leg or arm had a spasm. While I did have enough sense of touch that if someone poked me, I could feel it, there was no distinction of sharp or dull or hot and cold.

On a typical day, I would wake up and have my attendant prop me up in bed for a while. I developed the habit each morning of praying for the people I knew at that time. When I felt some energy, Patty would help me get ready for the day and I would decide what to have for breakfast. I'd have a cup of coffee with Jeff while my attendant prepared breakfast and fed me and then I would read or watch TV until lunchtime. If Jeff was working in the garage, he would join me for lunch. On a nice day, I would be wheeled out onto the deck to enjoy the garden and the sunshine. I couldn't stay in the sun too long, so I would need to be moved to the shade or brought in. Sitting out there would make me thirsty, and my attendant would hold up a straw so I could take sips of water. Then I would plan dinner and direct my attendant in making it.

When Jeff came in, I would say, "I made you dinner." Obviously, I didn't make it with my own hands, but I still felt like I had been responsible for making it happen. I planned the menus, dictated the shopping list, and instructed the attendant on what to do. I felt like I had made it. In some ways this attitude has to do with having self-esteem, recognizing that I was responsible for getting tasks done, even with the help of attendants, which gave me a sense of purpose. One time, I got a bunch of girls together and we made Christmas ornaments for Mel's teachers. My attendant drove me to the store, and I picked out the supplies, which my attendants put in the cart and brought home to set up. They helped the girls cut and glue. As the girls made the ornaments, I watched and offered suggestions. If you asked me, I would still say I did it. That doesn't mean that I didn't recognize all that my attendants did for me. I knew that the only way I would be able to do anything was with the help of another person. I was grateful beyond measure for every attendant who helped me over the years. I can't say often enough that they were and are my lifeline. But I needed to feel some self-determination over my life, or I wouldn't have the willpower to start a single day. My self-esteem was built on my ability to accomplish, so I had to adjust how I saw my accomplishments. Over time, this became easier.

Just like most women, I took on the mental load of running the household, keeping track of what had to be done, making sure it was done the way I wanted, knowing where everything was, planning menus and schedules, and keeping track of the calendar. My mom was usually there to help me, along with my attendants. Just because these tasks weren't completed with my hands doesn't mean I didn't do the work of getting things done. I was more of a manager than a doer. But I was truly a homemaker in that I was creating a home that was welcoming and comfortable for me and Jeff, for Mel, and even for my attendants. I was creating a home where people would gather and feel welcomed. For that reason, when I made dinner, I always made enough for extra people. I never knew who might stop by.

Even so, I got bored with it. I had been on a track as a successful professional. I had been socially and physically active. Running a house wasn't part of my strengths—it wasn't something I especially enjoyed. Nor did I see it as a way to live up to my vow to find a way to make my life feel meaningful.

———

When I made the list of three things I would do to live my life that day in the hospital, my reality still hadn't registered. It was one thing to say that I was paralyzed, but I had no idea what it would be like to be unable to move by myself. I didn't understand the physical or emotional trauma that I would have to deal with. It took me at least eight years to adjust physically to the trauma my body had endured. Even now, every morning I open my eyes and realize I can't move, as though it is happening all over again.

If someone asked me how I felt, I could say, "I feel normal from the chest up. If you tap me on my shoulder or put your arms around my neck or kiss my cheek, it just feels normal. From the chest down, it feels like my body has fallen asleep." It seems so obvious and simplistic to say, but it took all of that time to adjust to needing someone else do everything for me. Sometimes with my girlfriends I felt like my old self, and I could briefly forget about my disability. They knew me before and treated me the same way they always had, which let me go back to being the person they always knew. But most of the time, it was right in my face.

I saved my energy for my friends, but mainly for my family. When we had Mel, I wanted to be sure we managed to be like any family and to have fun together. Jeff is and was a great father. Having him around was like living with a clown. He really had a special relationship with Mel when she was growing up. He was the kind of dad who got down on the floor to play. He played every kind of ball or chased her around and tickled her. He played dress up and wrestled.

For the first few years, we couldn't take Mel on big trips, but we had enough time to go out to the lake and enjoy the water. Sometimes Jeff would pick me up from my wheelchair and carry me into the water where he would lay me in the center of a giant floating raft. He and Mel could swim around me, and I could float, feeling the gentle waves of the lake undulating below me.

It was hard after those family weekends to let Mel go. Jeff wanted her to spend more time with us, but the courts at the time definitely didn't favor dads in custody disputes. When Mel was twelve, she told us, "I want to spend more time with you." She told her mom, too, but her mom wouldn't agree. Of course, Mel was worried and didn't want to leave her mom all alone, either, especially after she divorced Mel's stepfather. We felt that we could offer her a more stable home, so we decided to go to court, not to take full custody, but to get more time with her. The judge wouldn't change the custody arrangement. He said, "I don't see anything that her mother is doing wrong that would warrant changing the custody agreement." We left the courtroom that day deflated. But Mel wasn't going to be deterred. She told her mother, "I don't care what the judge says. I want to spend more time with my dad." After that, we worked out a joint custody agreement, so Mel was with us half the time.

I was so happy to have Mel with us, and to see how happy it made Jeff. We started having a morning routine. I had multiple attendants at that point, so whoever was on duty would come at eight in the morning and feed Mel breakfast. Then she had time to play with her Barbie dolls or other toys. I'd be awake but wouldn't get out until around noon. After my morning coffee, we would go outside, go to the park, or make our visits. I wanted to be sure we would see her grandparents, uncles, and cousins. Jeff's grandparents were still alive, and we visited them. Eventually we got around the accessibility issue by having a portable metal ramp that went up several stairs. Many years later, there was a wooden ramp built at Jeff's parents' home. In the summer, we could always just sit outside. We had trips to the beach or the zoo and signed her up for summer camps at the local museum. And Mel had friends over whenever she wanted.

That was around the time that one of our cousins, who was a psychiatrist, reported my sister Joanne and her husband to Child Protective Services for neglect of their kids. I knew she was struggling, but I didn't think the phone call was warranted. The kids had everything they needed: food, cars, nice clothes, a beautiful home. I knew Joanne and her husband drank, but I didn't think things had gone too far. No matter what I thought, her three kids were going to be taken from her home. There was no way Jeff and I could let my nieces and nephew go into foster care, so we took them in. Mel had a bedroom for when she came, we had another bedroom for the teenage girls, and my nephew had his own room in the basement.

I can say that I was still in the midst of my recovery even after four years. But maybe having the kids in the house livened it up a bit and forced me to focus on something other than myself. It's funny because when the social workers talked to my family right after the accident, they thought that I had the mental attitude of someone who had been injured for seven years. I was accepting about what my life was going to be about. About four years into it, I wasn't accepting. I thought, *Enough. Isn't there going to be a cure?* Even when I wouldn't admit it, somewhere in the back of my mind, I kept thinking, *This is just temporary.* I was always aware that I had a reason to wallow but didn't let myself get tempted. In moments alone when I felt discontent about my situation creeping in, I diverted my mind with prayer or with thoughts of the people I love. It was never easy to do this, and I was still at an early stage of practicing control over my thoughts, of using my mind to shape my world.

———

We had Mel half the time. Stephanie, who had stood up in our wedding, and her two siblings, the three teenagers, lived with us full-time, but they went to school for most of the day. Evenings and weekends were time for fun. I taught Mel and the other kids how to play backgammon and we held championships. The girls loved to do hair and makeup, just like I did when I was young, and I let them brush and style my hair and do my makeup. Mel was great at makeup and brushing my hair, which had grown so long. She had a lot of practice since her own hair was way past her waist.

In the evenings, everyone ate dinner together then did homework. They told me they never had to do homework when they were home, and they certainly didn't study for tests. I thought about my own time as a student. I had never been serious, but I had learned some things. Now I realized that what I had learned and what I could do with my brain and my memory were the only things that hadn't been taken from me. Education gained a new significance, and I wanted to make sure none of the kids took it for granted. When they got home from school, I would ask, "What work do you have? What do you have completed? How can I help you?" We would start projects ahead of time to make sure they would have plenty of time to finish. Just as that would have been a surprise to me in high school, it was a surprise to them. But it worked. They did better in school.

Having teenagers around meant big day-to-day adjustments that Jeff and I had to make in our lives. We went very quickly from having limited time with Mel to having four kids in our house, with all the demands, changes in routines, and loss of privacy that entailed. But it was a joy to have them, and I loved the teenage drama. Stephanie liked to hang around the most, and she eventually became one of my attendants, living with us to attend community college even after her brother and sister, who stayed with us for almost two years, moved back to their parents. She used to sit on the bed talking on the phone with her friends. I remembered my phone calls, with the secret code talk about leadership when my dad listened in.

Stephanie didn't have any of those worries, and I got to see teenage life secondhand through her. Nostalgia for the past is a sweet and dangerous thing. For anyone, there is an element of longing, especially since it's easy to glamorize the past. I made sure to stay in the present, enjoying the funny quirks and special connection we had. One time, I overheard Steph talking to a friend whose dad was a director at the Civic Theater. She said, "Oh, that audition's today? I don't think I can sing or dance *today*."

"What?" I said. "You can't sing or dance any day." We both laughed. The lighthearted teasing of my brothers lived on.

"Well, my friend said if I try out, I can be in the chorus no matter what," Stephanie told me. She went to the audition but decided to be an usher instead of performing on the stage.

We were all pretty relieved about that decision. "Now I don't have to go hear you sing. So, I've got that going for me, which is nice," I teased her after opening night. That was one of my favorite quotes from *Caddyshack*.

Then there was the time we noticed all the washcloths were missing. We hunted through the laundry and looked all over the house. Washcloths were a weird thing to lose. "Where are they going? Down the drain?" I asked Jeff.

"I have no idea. Who uses them all?" Jeff asked.

Eventually the mystery was solved. Every morning, my niece would get a warm washcloth and take it with her in the car on the way to school to press on her face before she did her makeup. Then she would just toss it in the back seat. I can't imagine how that car smelled with its horde of damp cloths. I barely wanted them when she finally brought a pile back into the house to do the laundry. "You're in a load of trouble," I said. It took her a second, but eventually she caught on to the pun. There's a laugh in every situation if you look hard enough.

All in all, we had fun. When one of the kids couldn't concentrate on work, I would say, "Be the ball, Danny. Be the ball." We would laugh, but they'd get the point—concentrate on what you're doing until it becomes part of you. They started to quote other lines from our favorite movies, like *Caddyshack*. At dinner, someone was bound to say, "You ordered lunch to my room." And a kid would respond, "I knew that's where my mouth would be," from *Fletch*. The important thing was that we had meals together, which really was the center of family life.

We would tease Melisa a little, too. She was a perfectionist. Even if I wanted to be a perfectionist, I couldn't. There was no way I could expect that so much of my life was in control that I could have everything exactly as I wanted it. When Mel returned from her mom's house, as she walked down the hall, I would say, "Now don't get upset, but we dusted while you were gone, and somebody probably moved something." I thought I should try to help her loosen up. I already knew how life didn't fit into the neat and tidy box of our expectations. If you aren't too rigid, it's easier to accept all the challenges and joys that life can throw at you.

———

The movie version of my life would have a huge moment, an epiphany. All of a sudden, I would have some grandiose experience, and from that point forward, my body would start to heal, the pendulum of my emotions would stop, and I would settle into acceptance, if not contentment. Reality isn't that neat, of course. But I cannot extol enough the healing power of those little moments with the people who I loved sitting around as a family laughing, sharing meals, playing games. In some ways, it felt like a miracle that I could enjoy those things. I would look over at Jeff, laughing and goofing around with the kids, or catch a smile, or hear their excitement when they passed a test or got a grade that was higher than expected. I loved to say, "Oh honey, I'm so proud of you." I'm not saying I didn't want more from life, but I definitely treasured these moments and realized they were the true elements of a meaningful life.

Around this time, I got a call from Blodgett Hospital. They had a young lady in the hospital with a spinal cord injury. She was on a ventilator, and they were working to clear her to go to Craig Hospital in Denver, just as I had. Her doctor asked me if I could meet her and talk to her. Of course, I agreed. Jeff drove me over there. When I got to her hospital room, we had a nice visit. It was a stark reminder of just how far I had come. I thought, *I have a life. I have a husband and a family. I still have my girlfriends from high school and college. I have meaningful volunteer work.*

I told her about my life because I wanted to give her hope. I told her I was volunteering, and I still loved to garden. It wasn't the same as before, I told her, but I still had a social life. I remembered my days in the hospital when I had struggled on my own to envision a life after leaving and tried to tell her what I would have wanted to hear—not to fill her with false hope, but to let her know there was real hope. She went to Craig and when she came back, she got a downtown apartment and a job with the Girl Scouts. She had attendants who helped her get up and out in the mornings and back to bed at night. Later, she told me that the day I went to see her was pivotal in her recovery. For once, she said, she could see that after all the tubes and injections and doctors and therapists, she could build a life for herself. Sometimes seeing is believing.

Even though she was a virtual stranger, my visit to this young woman in the hospital may have been a pivotal point in my recovery, too. In a few seconds, I relived where I had been and how far I had come. The most important thing I could convey to her was that she could still have relationships with others, relationships built on friendship and love. My connection to others had always been significant to me, and telling someone in the same situation about my life made me feel proud and even a little relieved that I had stayed the same person at my core. I could see how focusing on what I could do had helped me do quite a lot.

———

Married Life: The Good, the Bad, and the Ugly, But Mostly Good

If I had to describe Jeff and me together, I would call us the Bickersons. We enjoy the combination of humor and competitiveness that comes out in a little playful bickering. I have a little advantage, because from my level, I can see everything, so when Jeff gets talking and I don't agree with what he is saying, I'll tell him, "Jeff, zip up your pants, you'll have more credibility." That usually stops him for a second, so he can check. I'll follow up with, "Quit while you're ahead." Then he'll say something to me like, "Well, Mary, you're not the boss here." But we both kind of know that isn't true. Even at six, our grandson JJ said, "Grandma is the boss of everything." On the other hand, Jeff uses this to make me the bad one. He'll tell JJ, "Be careful not to break that. It's Grandma's." Or "Grandma will be mad if you do that." I say, "I don't even know what he's talking about. Have fun." And they do because Jeff still plays with JJ the way he did with Mel. I call them Loud and Louder.

But the truth is that without a strong marriage, my life wouldn't be possible. Because of my injuries and the way I have to rely on Jeff, we have to be more aware of our marriage, more aware of communication, of our interdependence, of the need to keep romance alive. These are issues that all people in marriages have to struggle with, but because Jeff is not only my husband and friend, he is my caretaker, we have to be especially attentive to our marriage.

There's a reason JJ thinks I'm the boss of everything. I spend all day telling people what to do and how to do it. That's not just in my capacity as a board member of several charities and my ongoing role at Kids' Food Basket, where I am an active part of promoting the organization and fundraising. I'm also doing it all day long in our home, whether having an attendant open the door so I can go out on the deck or arrange the papers on my desk. And Jeff has been my attendant for the longest and for the largest part of the day. It's true he can in most cases anticipate what I need, so I don't have to ask, which is a relief sometimes. But I have to ask for a lot.

I've learned over the years to be absolutely clear about what I need and how I need it done. That's true with attendants, and it's also true with Jeff. He has learned to listen carefully. And out of respect for that, I listen carefully when he tells me what he needs. We have to communicate better than a normal couple because of my reliance on help with everything I do. There is so much uncertainty in my life, so much that is out of my control, that being able to express clearly what I need lets me regain a little of that feeling of autonomy, no matter how fragile. Because he takes care of my bodily needs, we are connected through physical intimacy, creating an even deeper commitment than we would have had if we were a "normal couple," as I call everyone else not in my or a similar situation.

Someone has to be with me all the time, and often that someone is Jeff. When it's not, that means we have an attendant present at all our daily interactions. It's true they might leave the room to take care of a chore, but there isn't a lot of privacy. That means the dynamics of our household are changed slightly. It's like always having a silent referee somewhere in the house. We are probably a bit nicer to each other than we might be if left alone all the time, even with our playful bickering. That shapes the habit of interaction, and once you establish a good habit, it's simple to carry it over to other aspects of our lives.

Because I depend on Jeff so much, it's an uphill battle to maintain our sense of romance. Luckily, we both are extremely demonstrative. I think if you are a person who is unaccustomed to or unable to express your feelings it's probably more difficult to maintain that aspect of your relationship after the initial burst of infatuation transforms to more mature love. The truth is that when we were in the first flush of our marriage, I was still healing from my injuries. I was tired a lot, and Jeff had to get used to my being too exhausted to go out with him. When I had someone else to be with me, Jeff went out with his friends. Also, he was incredibly busy building his business. Sometimes it was all we could do to share a kiss and a conversation about how we were doing before he carried me to bed.

We have had a long life together and have learned that romance can be about the simple gestures that show our love and care for each other. I might surprise Jeff by planning to take him out to dinner. Or I might have an attendant pack a picnic of our favorite foods, and Jeff will drive us to a lovely park, and we will have that time in nature, or sometimes our own deck and backyard. That's all we need.

When I wake up in the morning, I'll ask Jeff, "Where's the coffee?" Every morning with a wonderful smile, my husband brings me a cup of coffee. We drink a cup together and talk while my attendant makes breakfast. He used to make such weak coffee, but over the years he has adjusted to my taste, which shows me he's paying attention. During the day, he has to take care of running the errands for us both. When he goes to the bank to get cash for me, he always brings it home in an envelope. He writes nice little messages like, *For my sweetheart* or *To my hunny bunny*. I have saved those over the years. One time we were having a disagreement, and he only wrote *Mary* on the envelope. *I guess he's really mad at me,* I thought. I didn't save that one.

But when he talks to me or about me, Jeff is always loving and supportive. He compliments me and shares in my joys and triumphs, as I do for him. I've had more than one woman say to me, "I wish my husband talked about me the way Jeff talks about you."

"He should," I tell them. There's never a time when you can't say something loving and kind. "And you should talk about your husband that way, too."

Having fun together is also a way to keep romance going. Jeff is funny and loves to tell stories, and he keeps me laughing. I'm his fact checker. We love to entertain friends in our home and when he's talking, I'll see them look over at me, just to make sure he isn't telling tall tales, and I'll say, "That's BS." Sometimes I even get the chance to say, "Yes, that actually happened." We each bring something different to the relationship. In simplest terms, I'm the brains and he's the body. He's handsome, charismatic, and generous. He makes up goofy songs, dances around the house, tells his stories, and keeps everyone entertained. If I were with someone who was boring, that would be the worst. But someone who is laughing, excited, ready to travel, who keeps a spark in life, that's a person I want to be with.

Although we have a set of deeply held shared values, Jeff and I don't always agree. I wouldn't want to be in a marriage with someone who just agrees with me all the time. Or says he does when he doesn't. That feels patronizing. Because I have a disability, it can be tempting for people to defer to me because they feel sorry for me. I could capitalize on that in the way I might have done with a few tears when I was younger. But I don't want to set the stage for pity or special treatment, beyond what is absolutely necessary.

Sometimes we argue because we have different world views. Jeff thinks we should all take care of ourselves. I think it's a big world out there and we all need to take care of our global community. We all need to fight for world peace and equity for all people. He wouldn't even vote if it wasn't for me. I've talked him into voting and into what it is important to vote for, I'll admit. One time he asked me, "Are we going to vote for someone who wins this time?" I guess I like the underdog. It might be a popular position to claim to care about others, but when it comes down to action, not everybody follows their professed values, which means the underdog is often the one who is fighting for those important issues.

Just like any couple, we have our ups and downs, our agreements and disagreements. Unlike other couples, we have no choice but to be a team. We can't get into an argument and ignore each other for days. Jeff can't storm out in anger, and I certainly can't. My survival is important to both of us, not just to me. Jeff could never let me suffer alone; he loves me too much and is invested in our relationship. We had to find the balance and it wasn't easy. I need a lot from him, and he needs flexibility from me, so he doesn't burn out. We're together so much out of necessity. When one of us is empty and tired, we have to find ways to fill ourselves back up. I make sure he has time out with friends or takes a day to go for a motorcycle ride. He has friends from body-building and martial arts, which he's kept up through the years. He started teaching martial arts to kids with special needs; this way he has his own community as well.

I need some time away from him, too. I invite friends over for coffee or sometimes my former attendant Brad, who is an excellent chef, will call and say, "I want to throw a dinner party for you and your fun friends. You invite them and I'll come over and fix you a fancy dinner."

I truly believe that it isn't good for a couple to be constantly together, always involved in the same activities and interests. That's not a realistic situation for most people. We all have our unique needs and having to shape them to the needs of another can make life less fun. I mean, I guess if a couple truly wants to only do things together, God bless them if that is how they want to live their lives. But I believe each member of a couple needs outside interests. Jeff is more interesting if he goes out to a concert or movie and then comes back and we talk.

In general, my advice to young people who are getting married comes down to two things: give each other the benefit of the doubt and laugh together. In the heat of disagreement, people say a lot of things. Maybe they mean them, maybe they don't. If your partner says something that hurts your feelings, assume they didn't mean it. They want to express their true feelings, they want to describe a situa-

tion that needs to be improved to strengthen the relationship, or they are dealing with their own issues of past hurts
and personal preferences.

I remember one time when Jeff said something that hurt
my feelings. I don't even remember what he said, but I
remember the pain, like a hole in my heart. In those situations, it's tempting to strike back, to exchange hurt for hurt.
I have seen people do that, and I know that year after year,
those episodes build up until they become normal, and the
result is either extreme unhappiness, divorce, or both. There
was no way I would let that happen to us, so when Jeff hurt
me, I had to take a close look at the situation. I had to use
the communication skills we had been building throughout
the years. I told him that I understood him to be saying
something hurtful and it made me feel bad. He said, "That
isn't what I meant to say. I would never hurt your feelings."
That went a long way toward filling the hole in my heart.
The conversation afterwards helped us clear things up. We
can disagree, but we can do so with care and compassion.

Laughter can take you a long way, too. It helps that Jeff
is easy going and lighthearted. He loves to clown around.
When he's taking care of my physical needs sometimes he'll
sing me a funny little song. Or when I was watching the
Olympics, he came out into the living room in his under-
wear and did an ice-skating routine across the floor just to
make me laugh.

"Now you're a figure skater?" I asked. "You're about
eight inches taller and way lighter than any of them." I love
to laugh, and he loves an audience. The fact that we laugh
together has really been what has kept our marriage as

wonderful as it is. It would be easy to sink into darkness and just let our troubles and the troubles of the world weigh us down and make us negative. But we recognize too much that is good in our lives to let that happen. We have to make sure that we find some way to celebrate every day. And laughing together is one of the simplest ways to do so.

————

The changes in my physical state changed my mental state. The way I looked at life and my expectations had to be entirely revised once I no longer had the physical ability to do everything I wanted. Before I was injured, I expected to have three or four kids and to have a marriage very similar to my parents, each with our own set of interests and responsibilities, but coming together to build a life.

After we settled into married life, Jeff and I thought about adopting. We went through the whole process and attended classes for adoptive parents. On the last night of the class, we went home, and I felt a mixture of hope and apprehension. The classes had highlighted all of the responsibilities and expectations, and it felt like there would definitely be more to adopting than having more of our own children, if that were possible. And all of that was complicated further by my situation. I wouldn't be able to feed a baby or hold a baby. I wouldn't be able to lift a baby from a cradle or take a baby for a walk in a stroller. I could have attendants act as my arms and legs to do those things, but most of the time it would be Jeff. We sat in our living room, considering our options.

Finally, I said to Jeff, "I know I'm a lot of work. And having kids will be even more work for you. If you feel like it's too much, we don't have to do this."

"It feels like a lot," Jeff said. He had to be honest with me because the foundation of our relationship was communication. We wouldn't survive as a married couple, and I wouldn't survive at all, without it.

"We have Mel, and we have our nieces and nephews. There are enough children in our lives for us to love."

It's kind of funny that Mel became my daughter. When she was dating and about the age of getting married, I said to her, "I suppose you try to date guys who don't have kids."

"Yeah, I try," she said.

"I used to try to date guys who didn't have kids, and then I did, and the kid was you."

"Wow," was all she said.

She had such high expectations. "What I'm trying to say is that you're unrealistic about men," I told her. But she knew what she wanted, so she came to us one day and said, "I want to have a baby. I'm going to try an intrauterine insemination procedure. If it works, that means I'll be a single mom. What I want to know is if I will have your support and help."

"We have your back," we told her. "Whatever you need we'll give you."

"I'm so relieved," Mel said. "I have friends in the same situation, and their families would not be as supportive."

I knew I didn't want Mel to be in the same situation. I knew what it was like to have to consider if having a kid was a possibility or not. Over time, it has become easier, but it is heartbreaking. I console myself with the kids who I have had in my care and those whose lives I made better. What I didn't know was what a lifetime full of joy Mel's decision would bring us. JJ, our grandson, is the new love of my life. Just like when Mel was young and our nieces and nephew lived with us, the house is full of joy and laughter. We pick him up from school each day and watch him until Mel is done with work. I've taught him to play backgammon and he moves my pieces for me. I've watched Jeff roll around on the floor, roughhousing with him. When I cough, he runs into the room, pushes on my lungs, and says, "I got this," in his sweet little voice.

———

Fun with Friends: I Am Swung Through the Air (Or, I Sing Better after a Few Drinks)

Jeff and I are both extroverts, so being with people is one way we both are revitalized. I love to try out some of the recipes I find and share them with my friends, so we frequently have dinner parties on our deck. I like to make the recipes I've seen on the Food Network, something new and special, like roasted lamb, or something traditional like meat pies.

We also have a number of friends who are chefs and restaurateurs, along with my former attendant Brad. For almost 30 years we have had a loving, wonderful relationship with another couple, the Dills, who managed the Schnitzel-bank, a German restaurant. They prepare a fabulous meal a few times a year, doing all the cooking in their home, and then bring everything to our house. We often include over a dozen people. We have invited Lois, the widow of Norm Ginebaugh, one of the key donors at God's Kitchen and Kids' Food Basket. Norm was amazing because he volunteered 40 hours a week for many nonprofits around the community. We also have invited staff from Kids' Food Basket, along with Mel, Carol, and other dear friends. It's a wonderful time with stories and laughter, wine and a several course meal, including dessert. I'm careful about setting a beautiful table with fresh flowers. We all sit on the deck enjoying the lovely summer nights.

We also take trips with friends. My attendants join us, and though they are there to help me, they are part of the group as well. It is part of my dedication to taking care of the people who take care of me. It's so easy to get locked into a one-way relationship, and I try to be careful that doesn't happen.

We have an annual Mount Mercy friends' trip to a place on Brooks Lake. The house is an old brothel, so it has lots of rooms for a bunch of us. It's not entirely accessible, though, so Jeff and I always have a room on the first floor. We spend the week riding the pontoon boat, relaxing by the lake, and going to the nearby casino at night. Sometimes we have a bonfire.

I love to bring treats for my friends, a way of showing my love and care for them. I bring my famous blueberry French toast and some gourmet dips and breads and crackers. Sometimes I try some experiments with foods, and so far they've all turned out pretty well. Thank you, Food Network. There's a lot of alcohol floating around, so I don't know if anybody would notice or say anything if I made a meal that was truly bad. Mostly we just talk. One time one of our friends from high school brought a karaoke machine. I love to sing, even though I know I sound awful. I think I might sing better with a few drinks in me. For a while, Mel and my attendants would take me around to local bars to sing Karaoke, so I had some practice. My go-to Karaoke songs are anything by the Beatles, or "Sitting on the Dock of the Bay" or "Build Me Up Buttercup." I can say that I wasn't the worst singer in the bunch.

Fifteen years after we graduated high school, we got together and rented the Khardomah Lodge in Grand Haven, near Lake Michigan. As usual, there was a lot of alcohol. My friends were able to act as my attendants since they were used to helping me with regular tasks. When it was time for bed, my friends thought they could handle it. They wheeled me into the bedroom and all of them worked together to pick me up from my wheelchair. With the amount of drinking we had done, I'm surprised anybody was able to. Somehow, they decided it would be fun to swing me into the bed. Everyone was laughing and stumbling around. With some of them holding onto my feet and some of them holding onto my shoulders, they swung me back and forth like a hammock. One, two, three, then the old heave ho, and they tossed me onto the bed. We were laughing so hard it's amazing that they managed to land me right in my spot with my head on a pillow. The next morning nobody could believe what they had done. "I can't believe how much you trusted us," said Maria. "That was really gutsy." That's just what I wanted to be. Gutsy.

Jeff and I bought a pontoon boat, and Jeff would push my wheelchair down the dock and up the ramp to wedge me in place next to his captain's chair. We could ride around the lake and enjoy the sunshine. Just like in my childhood at our family cottage, I could bask in the sun and feel the warmth on my face. I could feel the faint breeze laden with the scent of the lake wash across me, inhaling deeply to savor every sensation.

———

Another way I take care of the people who are important to me is by giving gifts. In fact, this combines some of my favorite things: shopping, decorating, and showing people how important they are to me. I love to give gifts for every holiday, but especially Christmas. There were days when my attendants would spend their entire shifts just wrapping gifts. Jeff doesn't Christmas shop, except for me, but he loves to be generous too, so we have an extensive list of people we buy for.

I like to have my attendants take me out shopping a couple of times a week, whether for groceries, gifts, or things we need at home, though I'm doing more and more online shopping, especially with a pandemic raging. Often something will catch my eye and my attendant will take it down off the shelf so I can take a closer look. If I think it's perfect for Mel, or Stephanie, or anyone else, it goes in the cart. Luckily big stores and most small boutiques are pretty accessible, so I can drive around even in aisles of glass and ceramics. It's harder with the electric wheelchair because it's bulkier, but we manage. This is why legislation is so important. If it weren't for requirements for accessibility, people like me would be trapped at home in most instances. You can say that there are fewer than three million Americans in wheelchairs, so all those accommodations only benefit a few. But that would trivialize the value of living a full life for those millions of people, and when we as a society say some life is worth supporting and some life isn't, we devalue all life. Plus, there are the family and friends of those people, and the revenue we bring to the economy. All our lives have a ripple effect reaching outward to the shores of existence. So, I go about my business and live as full a life as possible.

I love to find handmade items, those that show the artistry of the crafter. And I'm always on the lookout for gifts that are practical, sometimes things even the recipients didn't know they needed or would never find. There's nothing better than visiting friends and seeing their homes sprinkled with trinkets I've found or meeting up for coffee and seeing the scarf I gifted is the perfect accessory for an outfit. It takes time and effort, but the people I know are worth time and effort. I find I don't need to spend a lot or buy expensive gifts to make people happy. It's the thought that counts, and I am eminently capable of thinking. That's my superpower.

LAUGHTER IS THE
BEST MEDICINE

You must do the thing you think you cannot do.

— ELEANOR ROOSEVELT

My attendants act as my arms, hands, and legs, doing the things I want to do that my body can't. The thoughts and impulses in my brain cannot be carried to my body through my spinal cord, but they can be conveyed to others via my voice. I get things done, but not the way able bodied people do. I need help, and I have to admit it and ask for it, which is something I can do better than most able bodied people. The similarity is that I have a vision for how I want my life to be, and I have to do whatever I can to make that vision a reality. The responsibility falls on the individual, even if we all need help to do the work.

Back row, left to right: Ashley Bodell, Brian Curran, Julie Riedy. Second row: Camillia Amash, Anna Sonnett, Emma Loveland, Melissa Shea, Janet Newman, Olivia Kukla, Nancy Mick. Front row: Sydney Hain, Theresa Blakely, Mary K. Hoodhood, Melisa Hoodhood.

If able bodied people had to list all the things they do for themselves during the day, they probably wouldn't be able to. Most likely, they aren't even aware of half of them. I am acutely aware of the smallest task but have learned not to be afraid to say, "I need this." And to say please and thank you. I say thank you every day, all day long, because I don't take anything for granted. My attendants are my whole life. Without their help and support, I would just be a pretty face sitting helplessly in a bed, unable to even get myself into a wheelchair. I live every day with an overriding sense of gratitude and love for them.

Through the years I have had many family members and friends as attendants, and many of my attendants who didn't start out that way have become our family. There is no doubt that it is an intimate relationship, whether the role is being filled by Jeff or by others, and I have had to be comfortable with intimacy in a way that many people never are. I see every day how all our lives are interconnected, only possible with the support and help of others, whether an extreme case like mine or in less obvious ways for able bodied people.

With technology, I start my day in small ways by myself. I can use my Echo to turn on the television or make a few phone calls. The bedroom I share with Jeff is more like a living room, and I frequently have people congregated around my bed for meetings or visits. But I have to have an attendant use the remote control to operate my bed, lift me into my wheelchair, brush my teeth, wash my face, apply moisturizer and makeup, brush my hair. I need help, usually from Jeff, to be lifted into the shower seat and to go to the bathroom.

I like to get things done, so I am usually multitasking, and it helps to have an attendant who can keep up and who knows what needs to be done. If I'm reading a magazine and my hair falls in my eyes or I need a page turned, I have to ask. I have to remember a lot because I can't just do things myself. When Stephanie is visiting and wants to use my curling iron, for example, I can't just walk over and riffle through a drawer or cupboard to find it. I have to be able to say, "It's in the top left corner of the linen closet above the towels and below the sheets." Or whatever.

It's good to have an attendant who already knows how to do things, but I'm willing to teach them. My work recruiting and training volunteers for God's Kitchen and Kids' Food Basket helped me with this, or perhaps it's the other way around. When Brad started working for me, he was a teenager. He had an interest in cooking, so we tackled complicated recipes that we found on our favorite cooking shows. I might have had to explain what it meant to julienne carrots or sauté onions at first, but he was able to take over a lot. That left me free to do the things I needed to do.

When I was at home and Jeff was building his business, my attendants did the household chores I would have been doing. It's important to me to have a comfortable, welcoming home, and I couldn't do any of it without my attendants. They vacuum and dust—and it helps if they can see the dust in the corner rather than having me point it out. Maybe they have to serve a little bit as my eyes, seeing the world I see and helping me shape it to what I need. As I have said, it is the mental load of running a household that most women tire under. Some of the time, I get so tired that I'll just say, "I feel so lazy. I don't even feel like giving directions."

I have definitely learned to deal with frustration and with waiting. Nobody can do what you want when you want as fast or in the same way as you would do it yourself. My friend Cindy was caring for her mother and mentioned her mom wanted everything exactly her way. I could only reply, "I learned to give that up a long time ago. I'm just happy if it is done." Of course, there have been times when I have lost patience, but I keep trying to do better. I'm aware that I wouldn't have lived or had as good a life as I have had without my attendants' care. It's just that even if I say they are acting as my arms and legs, they aren't the same as my own arms and legs.

Most of my attendants have been female, but I have had a number of caring and nurturing men as attendants, too, including Jeff. Along with Brad, Brian was with me for a long time. He stepped forward when JJ was born, since Jeff and I had committed to being available for Mel. As an attendant he was immersed in my whole life and that of my family, helping to take care of JJ from the time he was an infant. Most of the personal things are taken care of by Jeff or some of my female attendants, but Brian even learned how to put on my makeup. I can see him sitting across from me with the mascara wand, hands a little shaky. Or carefully drawing a bow on my lips with one of my favorite lipstick colors.

Brad, who now works for Kids' Food Basket, grew up with Stephanie because his mother and my sister Joanne were best friends. We met at some of the pool parties Joanne used to throw. Stephanie was already working as an attendant for me, but we needed extra help to cover some hours, so Brad joined us. He worked with me for a long time, on and off, and still travels with us on vacations. I like people who are funny and cool. If you have to rely on them and make them part of your family, it really makes sense to like them and enjoy their company. When we are entertaining or having dinner, we like to treat our attendants the same as our other guests. Jeff will pour them a drink, and I'll invite them to the table. They take part in the conversation. I like to say, "If you are part of my life, you are part of my life." I want to welcome them and create a human relationship, the kind of give and take I want from all the people I meet.

One of the biggest parts of the job is meals. Three times a day, plus every snack or sip of water that I need. Attendants prepare these, with my planning and instructions, and they serve them to me. Whether we're alone or with a group of friends, at home or at a restaurant or an awards dinner, my attendants—including Jeff and sometimes the friends I am out with—have to cut up my food and feed it to me. Over time, attendants get more used to this. They know I like smaller bites and a mix of flavors. They know when I'm immersed in conversation they should wait before putting a forkful of food in my mouth. Of course, there are mess ups. I'll get a bite that's too big for me to chew or they'll drop food on me. It's always my favorite blouse, of course. But I can't blame them or get upset. It's better to have them spread a napkin over me. It's unusual to be in public and see an adult being fed, so some people gawk. That's not my problem, and I assume if we all act like it's natural, they'll get used to it.

Since I got out of rehab at Craig Hospital, my most faithful and constant attendant has been Jeff. If I didn't have my other attendants, everything would fall on him, and I don't think he would do well by himself. I don't think he would manage keeping a household running—though you never know how someone might rise to the occasion. Jeff doesn't like it when I tell him what to do, like I do with other attendants, especially when it comes to housework. He wants to do it on his own in his own way. Keeping the balance between my need for his care and my need for a husband is tough, but somehow we've managed all these years, mostly by keeping a sense of humor.

Jeff is amazing, and I know he is the main reason I am still alive. One time we had an appointment with the eye doctor and needed to leave home at 1:30. At 1:05, we had an appointment to call our insurance agent. As I was getting dressed, we realized my catheter must have leaked. It could have been a crisis, even without the impending appointment. In 25 minutes Jeff changed the tube, got me in my shower chair and even washed my hair while my attendant Libby stripped and changed the bed. After all that, we made it to the eye appointment on time. I was talking to my friend Carol later in the day, and she said, "Imagine if he wasn't here."

"I don't even want to think about it," I replied.

Adaptive Technology: Doing What I Can't Do for Me

For most people, having an Amazon Echo can be a convenience, just like a dishwasher or a Roomba. Technology takes care of the things they need to do but don't have time or inclination for. For me, on the other hand, technology gives me the smallest amount of independence, of the sense, however fragile, that I have some control over my life and what I do. Having adaptive technology cuts down on what I have to ask of Jeff and my attendants.

But technology isn't always easy to embrace. When I was sent home from Craig Hospital, I didn't want an electric wheelchair. I can't say it makes sense, but it just seemed like too much to handle at the time. And it felt like I would be calling more attention to myself. Looking back, I think having the manual wheelchair made me more patient. I had to wait for someone to push me to get where I needed to go. I had that manual wheelchair for a couple of years and developed the habit of praying or meditating while I waited for help.

Then I went for a rehab evaluation at Mary Free Bed Hospital. The therapist mentioned they had a power pack, a little motor clamped onto the back of the manual wheelchair, to convert it into an electric wheelchair. That lasted eight years. I liked it enough that the next time, I bought an electric wheelchair thinking that would be even better. The real reason I went to the electric wheelchair was that I wanted more independence, especially when I was gardening. I could move to different parts of the garden as I wanted. If I saw that one spot needed more soil, I could navigate to the garage, have Jeff pile it onto my lap and get the soil to an attendant waiting where I wanted it to go, feeling like I had done it myself. I had a real sense of accomplishment working in the garden, even when things didn't go exactly as I planned. I tried to cultivate vegetables, but the deer ate them. We tried apple trees, too. Deer again. But it didn't matter, I could always have flowers. I love flowers and being able to do part of the work of cultivating them gave me a real sense of accomplishment. When I can move around my garden and see the results of my efforts, I'm thankful for the wheelchair, and for the bit of control I gain over my surroundings.

The problem with the electric wheelchair was driving it.

Sure, in the manual chair, someone would push me into a wall from time to time, but it didn't happen that often. When I was the wheelchair driver, who knew where I would end up? I was born right-handed, but my right hand no longer worked. I had to rely on limited motion in my left shoulder to direct the chair. When I went to the doctor, she said, "Wow, you're really good at driving that."

"Yeah? Come to my house and get a look at my walls and my door jambs. Or the spot where I took a big chunk out of the brick by the fireplace." We had a little chuckle, but the truth is I am so glad to have the bit of independence I have gotten from my wheelchair.

When I first got it, Jeff would joke, "Mary K., I cannot believe you aren't running people over." Or, "Hey MK, there's a guy in a wheelchair. You want to show him you have one too?"

I can give as good as I get, so I just said, "Hey, Jeff, there's a guy over there who is an asshole. You want to go talk to him?"

I've also used adaptive technology to help me read a book or manual, operate the phone, and use the television. I used to have a Sip and Puff, technology that had been around since the 1960s. A Sip and Puff straw was attached to my phone at a level where I could reach it with my mouth. The device was connected to operate the landline phone and the TV. With a sip of air, I could turn the TV on or alert directory assistance for the phone. Then I'd just say, "Please call this number," and there I was, making phone calls. A puff of air would turn off the TV or hang up the phone. Now, voice activation takes care of so much more.

I used to have the software program Dragon Dictate. I found it difficult to use when I was in grad school trying to write papers. It felt like I had to use the same part of my brain to give commands to the program as I did to compose what I was writing. That just felt overwhelming. I decided I would dictate to my attendants since I was lucky enough to have them. Then I would be able to think better.

Every new development in technology has the potential to transform the lives of people with disabilities—if they have access to it and if they can afford it. What it comes down to is people. People have to see those of us who live on the fringe, recognize our shared humanity, and exert the will to make sure that every advantage is passed on to those who need it. This is true of people with disabilities, people who live in poverty, people with mental health needs, people who need nourishing food, and anyone who in some way pushes against the norms of society. I know it was easier for me to see all these people once I became one of them. To follow the Golden Rule and "Do unto others as you would have them do unto you," you have to be able to put yourself in others' places and understand what someone in that situation would truly want. It is easy to be flippant and say, "I would just do this, and I wouldn't have that problem." But the truth is that nothing is ever that simple, and until we make the effort and practice true empathy, there will always be suffering that could have been avoided. So much of the suffering is caused by humans, and it can be eased by us.

Public Reactions: You Don't Have to Talk so Loud

I was lucky that my friends and family continued to see me as a person, as myself. They even continued to tease me the way they always had.

Like when my brother Terry said to me, "Okay, Mary K., are you really injured or are you just trying to get all the attention?"

"Nope, I'm paralyzed. Isn't that a kick in the ass?" I said to him.

It could seem that Terry was being rough on me, but it would have been far worse if he had started treating me like I was fragile and in need of cosseting. And I always knew he loved me. There was the time Terry and his wife Pam, who are both cancer survivors, participated in Relay for Life. Terry invited me to the event afterward where he made a speech about being inspired by people around him, and he named me. That really made me smile.

But not everybody treated me the same. Most people with disabilities have to deal with other people staring and gawking. One of the reasons they took us out into the world during rehab at Craig Hospital was to get us used to the way people would react to us. I see three common reactions: 1) Oh, poor you. 2) I wonder what's wrong with you. 3) I'm glad it's not me. Maybe it's, "I wouldn't want to be you." I had to get used to people staring at me, the side glances and the little smiles. Especially from women, it felt to me. Seeing people's reaction to me undermined my sense that I was making progress, that I could lead a normal life. It undermined my self-esteem. I hadn't wanted to be the center of attention in that way. This is partly why I avoided an electric wheelchair at first. It seemed like the motor would be loud and the chair itself would be bulkier, calling even more attention to me. I didn't want to make a spectacle of myself. I had to train myself not to care, to ignore the stares and to focus on my actions and on what I wanted to do. Now, when I enter a room, I want people to pay attention because they respect me, not because they pity me.

Oddly, people talk extra loud to me, as though being in a wheelchair somehow also makes me hard of hearing. I know it's part of being uncomfortable around someone with a disability, not knowing how to behave, but it's still annoying. As they are yelling at me, I want to scream at them, "What the hell? Just treat me like a human being. Look past my wheelchair and see me. I can still think and talk. I'm still a person." I haven't screamed yet, but the temptation is always there. Instead, I used to try to say something profound and intelligent, so maybe they would see that my disability didn't extend to my brain. That was when I cared. Now I don't care as much. I concentrate on the people who know me.

Little kids have always stared. At first it was disconcerting. My immediate thought when I was out in public and a kid was rudely staring was, *All right you little brat, where's your mother? Why haven't your parents taught you any manners?* After Kids' Food Basket was going, I spent a lot of time in schools, meeting with kids and their families. Then I started talking to kids and realized they aren't looking at me, they are looking at my wheelchair. They want me out and them in. When they talk to me, it's always about how they can get one of their own because it looks like fun. I have to talk to them about the difference between *get* to and *have* to. Sometimes kids will look at my feet, like Mel did on her first visit to the hospital, and wonder why they don't work. This was especially clear to me with our grandson JJ. From the time he was a toddler, he loved to ride on my wheelchair, sometimes on my lap and sometimes on the footrests. One time I took him for a spin, and he flew off, almost running into a dresser. I didn't tell his mother until three years later.

The most surprising reactions come from doctors and other social workers. I've had many doctors who, when I get in their offices, talk to my attendant. "What's going on?" they'll ask the person standing next to me, totally ignoring my existence.

"What are you asking them for? They don't know," I'll say.

I had to make an appointment with a plastic surgeon. He originally wanted me to take an ambulance to be wheeled in on a gurney to his office. "Why make this an all-day ordeal?" I said. The only way he would see me without the ambulance was at the wound clinic where I already had an appointment with another doctor. He came into the examination room during my appointment. My doctor was looking at my back, so he had leaned me forward in my wheelchair. The first thing the plastic surgeon said when he walked into the room was, "Do you live in a nursing home?" He assumed I couldn't live anywhere else.

"Do you know about Kids' Food Basket?" I countered.

"Yes, my son's kindergarten just adopted them as their project."

"I'm the founder. And no, I don't live in a nursing

home." I wondered if he missed the class in sensitivity training or if he just relied on stereotypes.

At another appointment in a hospital a doctor asked, "When you are at home, do you go anywhere?"

"Do you mean outside?" I asked.

"No, do you go out?"

"Like in the community?" I asked. I couldn't believe he assumed I was locked in my house.

The point is that even doctors make assumptions based on stereotypes about people with disabilities. It's like they can shorthand getting to know you or your specific lifestyle, even when they might impact your care. Nobody, no matter what their circumstances, wants to be treated like a stereotype rather than an individual.

Again, I asked, "Do you know about Kids' Food Basket?"

"Yes, I was just talking to another doctor about it."

"I'm the founder."

"Oh, I get it now," he said. His implication was that I was different from other people with disabilities who didn't have to go anywhere. That's the kind of ridiculous assumption that makes accommodating people with disabilities so difficult, the kind of assumption I fought when I worked for Disability Advocates. This pervasive attitude is why it is vital to have legislation that protects people who don't fit in the mainstream of society to allow them to live fulfilling lives.

Another time, as I was getting ready to leave the hospital, a social worker stopped in my room. "Do you have a way to get home? Do you have a plan when you get there?" I know it was her job, but did she fail to look at my chart?

"Yes, I'm a social worker, too," I said. "And I've been a quadriplegic for thirty years. I think I have a plan."

Of course, the good doctors and social workers far outnumber the insensitive ones. My doctors are some of my favorite people, even though I always tell them I'd rather be anywhere else than in a medical office. People in general think that people with disabilities don't have lives. I've been fortunate enough to be able to manage my disability in an efficient way. My health is good enough and I've had a support system, so that after the first eight years of recovery, I have lived a reasonably happy life. I have met a lot of people with varying disabilities who have also managed well. I know that not everybody who has a disability is as fortunate, but the assumption that nobody is or can be happy is just insulting. It's just one more prejudice that humans heap onto each other, limiting possibilities, limiting human connection. I'll never understand why people do that.

———

Insurance: The Lord Giveth and the Lord Taketh Away

One thing my sister Joanne did that was really good was to work with the insurance company to get benefits that others didn't get. She was a smart, articulate businessperson who asked the right questions. Everyone should have an advocate like her on their side. I have had many lawyers, doctors, and insurance agents who say, "I don't know anybody who has all these benefits."

My advice to anyone facing this daunting situation is this: ask many questions, knowing you have the right to ask.

It goes back to listening, too, because by paying attention to what you are told, you'll know what benefits you're entitled to and what issues you need to pursue. You might have to fight to get what you need, and you might have to build a case for yourself. Instead of getting angry or taking things personally, try to be objective and offer evidence when you can. And if possible, find someone else to advocate for you when you don't have the energy to fight for yourself.

For instance, until the early 2000s, Jeff wasn't paid for nights or weekends. About 20 years ago, my case was sold from one insurance agency to another to process my claim with the Michigan Catastrophic Insurance Fund. The new adjustor was awful. That motivated me to get a lawyer, who wrote a letter demanding they pay for the 24 hour care I required. Up to this point, even though I knew I needed around the clock care, I was still trying to be independent. Plus, we liked our previous insurance adjustor and wanted to work with him, so we didn't make as many demands.

After hiring the lawyer, it took two years, but when I won, Jeff was paid back to the day of discovery, from nine at night until eight in the morning. Jeff sleeps during this time, too, but he's what they call my safety backup. That means if I need to be moved during the night so I don't get bedsores, or if there were a fire, I would have someone to help me. In 2019, a new law went into effect that said a family member could not serve as an attendant for more than 56 hours a week. We had to draw up a new contract that stated he is compensated for safety. The system has worked. It has been over 40 years since my injury, and I've only had a few major bedsores.

When my injury was 22 years old (yes, I know it sounds like it has a life of its own, and maybe that's so), and I was working at Disability Advocates, my insurance provider wanted to do an independent study. I know they wanted to figure out how long I would live, because my care is expensive. The insurance processor requested an independent audit. At Disability Advocates, my job included working with people wanting to get out of nursing homes and back into independent living situations. After having my own personal care attendants that I hire and train, I used what I had learned to help others do the same.

My lawyer said, "I know the doctor they're sending you to for the audit. He will give a bad report, so don't be in the room alone with him, and keep your answers short—just yes or no." This was one of the times in life I thought strategically. One of the smartest things I did was to have one of my attendants create a chart on the computer with 15-minute segments of what they do for me around the clock. I put the report in a folder and went to the doctor. Jeff came with me to the doctor's audit.

I kept in mind my lawyer's advice and stuck to yes or no answers. The doctor asked about my range of motion. Jeff is really good at anatomy from his time in bodybuilding and martial arts, so he was able to answer a lot of questions. When the doctor asked why I didn't rely on Jeff to cover more hours, I said, "He's my husband and I don't want to burn him out." The doctor conducted my physical. As I was getting ready to leave, I said, "Doctor, in case you didn't understand, I prepared this chart for you, so you have a 24 hour view of what my attendants do for me." My intent was that when he wrote his report, he would use my data—from my mouth to his ear, as they say.

Later that week, my lawyer called and asked, "What did you say?"

"Why?"

"I've seen a lot of reports from this guy. This is the first time I've seen him say anything positive. His words were, 'I've never seen anybody who is more in tune with their disability. Whatever she has been doing for the last 22 years, she should continue doing.'"

The upshot is that I judge from my own knowledge of what is going on and if I need help, I ask a lawyer. So, the best of my advice is this: Don't be afraid to ask a lot of questions and take notes. The people you are working with don't have the same investment in your life. You have to advocate for yourself, or, if you can't, find someone who can. Ask for everything, and hope to get it, but have a plan if you don't.

———

Travel: Yes, I Can Damn Well Leave my House

It's easy for outsiders to see me in my wheelchair and assume I'm locked in a little life in my home. It's likely that would be the case if I had lived at any other point in history, if I would have survived at all. While it takes a little more effort, and I can't go everywhere, I love to travel, to experience different places and people. We have managed trips to Mackinac Island, Traverse City, Chicago, Florida, California, Las Vegas, New York City, Washington, DC, Canada, and even Aruba.

We've made an effort to take Mel to see the United States. We got our first van in 1984. There was a lift for me to get in and out as well as a place to lock in my wheelchair, and seating for several other people. On longer trips we converted the bench seat in the back to a bed, and Jeff would lay me down in it as he drove. Since he worked with cars, he always made sure we had the best sound system and other amenities, so our van became a party van. We took Mel to Rhode Island when she was eleven. It was Mel, Jeff, Jeff's dad George, and me for a week. Jeff tied the luggage on the top of the van, but we didn't get too far before someone pulled up next to us and shouted through the window, "Hey, you lost a suitcase!" Mel's suitcase had flown off the top of the van on the highway! There was no way for us to retrieve everything, so we had to buy her all new clothes. "Well, I lost some of my favorite stuff, but I got some new stuff," she said. "So, I guess it worked out." I was glad to see that she was learning to take things as they happened, such an important lesson.

We took Mel to California for her fourteenth birthday and invited her best friend along. We saw San Diego and Venice Beach, where all the bodybuilders go. Jeff was in his element. He met Fred Ward from Remo Williams and David Rasche who played Sledge Hammer. One of our best trips was for Mel's 21st birthday, when we flew to Las Vegas. It was the three of us, plus my attendant Brad who was Mel's best friend by then. Jeff's friends Phil and Bob met us there. We flew on the day of her birthday, and Jeff told the flight attendants what day it was. The airline poured champagne for everyone in our section, and they all sang "Happy Birthday." The look of joy and excitement on Mel's face could fill my heart forever.

We've taken many trips to Florida, and the Keys, where a generous friend lets us use his condo. Brad was a regular attendant on these trips. One time, he went to get us drinks. Somehow, he tripped and spilled the entire drink over me. "What the hell are you trying to do to me?" I said, but he could see that I was laughing. "Just dry me off and everything will be fine." Bad things are going to happen. It doesn't make life better to get upset or angry. I've never had anyone intentionally hurt me, and I don't expect it, so I take every situation as an opportunity to enjoy a new sensation.

Of course, some places are more accessible than others, and beaches and pool decks are a challenge. We figured out how to put down boards to make a path. If we can find hard packed sand or paths, that makes things easier in my wheelchair, but especially when we were young, sometimes Jeff would just carry me out onto the beach and prop me in a lounge chair so I could enjoy the sunshine and the lapping of the waves on the shore. When I'd had too much sun, someone would move an umbrella around as needed. At our friend's condo there's a pool and Jeff will carry me out there and hold on to me so I can float around.

Our most frequent trips were probably camping in the area, especially Traverse City, Michigan, which is stunningly beautiful. My attitude had changed since that Fishing and Wildlife course. We were headed on a camping trip when we had the accident that caused my injuries, and we continued to camp afterward. I would make lists of everything we needed, and Jeff would pack up and do all the cooking. We would pull into the campgrounds where Jeff would set up the bonfire and the tent. Jeff and I slept in the bed in the back of the van while Mel and any other kids, if they were with us, slept in the tent. We cooked meals on the bonfire or the camp stove, roasted marshmallows and shared stories. Sometimes Jeff would dance around the campfire or tell funny jokes. Often friends would meet us—or we made new friends there—and we soon had crowds of people laughing and talking, drinking, and eating around the bonfire.

Right across the street from the campground was a place where Jeff could put in jet skis or a windsurfer. He pushed the wheelchair as far as he could then picked me up, sat me on a blanket, and propped me up. I'd sit in the sun for a while and have someone move me into the shade. Jeff was windsurfing one time and got so far out he couldn't get back. I was nervous so I sent a friend of Mel's on a jet ski to pull him back in. I didn't want to lose him any more than he wanted to lose me.

Hospitalizations: Think of It as a Spa Day

In 2004, Jeff and I decided to brave going on a cruise, something I always wanted to do. At the time, I didn't know I had an abscess in my intestine. I thought I had a light case of flu and would get better. It ruptured when I was on the boat. People a lot stronger than me don't make it through such a thing. I woke up in a hospital in St. Thomas. It was the kind of place where hot water only came to the second floor, and I was on the third floor. A nurse from the States told Jeff he should get me out of there. It cost $25,000 to fly back to the United States in a private plane. We didn't have the money, so a friend lent it to us. Insurance later reimbursed us. The situation I put myself in was dangerous, but I didn't know because I couldn't feel pain the way an able bodied person would. I generally followed my mother's attitude toward illness: just eat some chicken soup and you'll be fine. I'm very careful, but I can't live my life in constant fear of getting sick.

When you have had catastrophic injuries and are paralyzed, you live with the threat of other health issues. The list the doctors gave me at Craig Hospital was long, but it didn't cover every complication I've endured. I spend a lot of my time in hospitals, and I've been very close to death a few times. Before Covid I would go to my urologist every year. I have chronic kidney stones, which are part of my disability. I had to go for treatment for years, until my urologist said we got rid of them. I still have to go for regular blood work.

So, I had to deal with what has happened to my body, but I also had to navigate the world. You would think that having one motor vehicle accident was enough. But in 2017, when I was at Mary Free Bed Rehabilitation Hospital for one of my regular checkups, I had another. My attendant at the time drove me there. When we came back out, someone had parked too close to the handicapped space so there wasn't room for the lift that would allow me to get back into the van. It takes at least six feet, which is why those handicapped parking spots have a wide area next to them designated for that purpose. Many people ignore that, and one of those people put me in a dangerous situation.

We waited for a while, but nobody came to move the car, so I told my attendant to back the van out so we would have room to lower the lift and I could get into the van. I waited on the side of the parking lot while she backed out, and a woman in another vehicle backed into me. She must have heard the sound as her vehicle hit my wheelchair. She just bumped me, but of course I couldn't feel the point of impact. But I felt the jolt. She knocked the pillows that prop up my arms and my feet to the ground.

She jumped out of the car, "I'm so sorry. My husband is in a wheelchair. I'm going to pick him up. I can't believe I hurt another person in a wheelchair." Even though I was right next to Mary Free Bed, they brought an ambulance. I didn't need that, so I just wheeled over to St. Mary's Hospital where I saw a physician's assistant. She said, "Your vitals are better than mine. It looks like there is no sore." My skin wasn't broken, but I had an interior bruise that opened up later on, leaving an injury three or four inches around, deep to my bone, above my waist. There was a gaping hole in my back and more medical bills. We eventually settled out of court for the payment of the bills. Even after everything was cleared up, it was one more reminder of how fragile my life is.

Before my injuries, if I had a sore neck or an ache or bruise somewhere, I thought if I waited long enough, it might just go away. Even now, I'm a procrastinator for my health in spite of the fact that I know more than anyone how precarious life is since I have been close to losing it many times. Feeling your own death breathing down your back has an eerie quality, like when you see a scary movie and you feel chills run through your body and a sense of the void on the outer edge of existence. Sometimes I get tired of the fight, thinking it might be easier to just go into the basement and confront the guy with the bloody ax and get this movie to its finale. But I know when I get there, I'm going to fight the guy with the bloody ax and most likely I am going to triumph.

But I wasn't always sure I would triumph. Once I was in the hospital on a ventilator and couldn't talk. I woke up and felt like crap. I had had another tracheotomy and couldn't talk. Jeff was lousy at reading lips, but my attendant Brian was there, and I had one of those Patient Communication Boards. I could communicate by shaking my head so he would know what letters to write down. He wrote down what I said: "Tell Jeff that if it's time to let me go, he needs to let me go."

"I'll write this down, but I'm not reading it to him," Brian said. He was emotional at the thought that I was ready to go if it was my time. He handed the paper to Jeff. Jeff looked at the paper.

"What are you talking about? You're getting better. You'll be out of the hospital in no time."

"Nobody told me," I said. Because I don't have feeling in my body, it's hard for me to distinguish when I am well and when I am really sick. I truly believed I was dying until Jeff reassured me.

When they took the trach tube out, I freaked out a little. Fortunately, Jeff was there and talked me through it.

"Mary K., they're going to take the trach out." He could

see I was worried. "They think you are strong enough." I hoped I was strong enough.

At that point, I felt exhausted and thought I was on the brink of death. Sometimes I just keep going for the people I love. When I'm feeling well enough to get out of the hospital, I tell the doctors, "I have a crazy Arab husband running around the North End who doesn't know what to do without me." Then they send me home and I start all over again.

In 1995, I made it through the year doctors had predicted would be my last. I remembered that day at Craig Hospital, sitting at the table with my mother, Patty, and Jeff. I remembered the doctors' statistics and the doctors' certainty. They told me a lot of stuff I didn't want to hear, and I just blocked it out—that was my coping mechanism. Still, 1995 was a year I approached with apprehension, knowing I had so much to live for. I had hope, and that got me through. In the reality of life, nobody is promised tomorrow. I learned to appreciate what I had. I got through that year because of love from Jeff and my family.

Again around the year 2000, I felt certain I wouldn't make it past 2010. I had already lived so much longer than the doctors predicted. I had either been in the hospital or was tired and recuperating for such a long time. I'd had kidney stones and collapsed lungs. But somehow I found the strength to keep going.

And it turns out that strength comes from someplace deep inside, from a place we don't always know is there. It's the will to live, to survive, to do more than survive. It's the will to make a life you want to live. It can get buried under all the burdens of life, but there's always a tiny window of light that seeps out from the darkness and can lead us to amazing things if we let it. I had always enjoyed life, so it's hard to say that being faced with death made me appreciate life. I do know that every morning when I wake up, after I have a moment to adjust to the world, I'm a little bit surprised and filled with gratitude for another day.

Recently, my brother Mike had to be hospitalized. I was talking to him on the phone, and told him, "I hate hospitals. The only way I get through staying at one is by pretending I'm at a spa where I get pampered, and everyone waits on me hand and foot." There was silence at the other end of the line. I could feel Mike thinking, trying to hold back the joke he wanted to make. I said it for him, "Yes, my whole life is having people wait on me hand and foot. Hell, I'm just lucky that way." I laughed so hard at myself that I could barely hear what he said. Pretty soon he was laughing, too. I hoped that laughter gave him a little boost in his recovery, just as laughter had always seemed to save me.

There's a cliche that says we have to experience the bad to appreciate the good. I'm not sure it's true, but I know my struggle to stay alive has changed my perspective on life. I know all life is worth living and every living being deserves the chance to flourish. Did that give me the drive to start Kids' Food Basket and help keep it growing? I don't know for sure. I'd like to think that I would have done it anyway. Life is precarious, and the events in a life are subject to so much chance. We like to think we have control, but I got rid of that notion a long time ago.

Sorrows: The Love Never Dies

If life were fair, then after having such a traumatic event and becoming paralyzed, there would be no more suffering in my life. But if life were fair, I wouldn't have been in the damn accident in the first place. So, what I'm saying is life isn't fair. Not only did I suffer, but I've seen others around me suffer and die. I feel these losses deeply because every connection I have with another person secures my life and sustains my life in ways that are intricate, lovely, and vital. Before the accident, I had seen my father wither away and die after his stroke. I was grateful every day to have my mom by my side until her death on December 3, 1986, the anniversary of her own father's death, 35 years earlier. I thought, *God loves her so much that He wanted her with Him.* That was small consolation, but I had to seek solace where I could. She had spent her last day with us playing Scrabble. Then she went home and played cards with my brother, my sister-in-law, and their daughter. She died that night in her sleep, as calmly and peacefully as she had lived her life. Like my dad, I think of her and miss her every day.

My sister Joanne died prematurely at 52. I couldn't believe it had happened. When she died, I went to counseling. I measure people on how they react to stuff, and counseling had definitely helped me learn to react in ways that are healthier. We can control our reactions, take things one step at a time, and figure out what we're going to do to offset the negative. Out of all the things we can't control, we can control that.

I've been to a helluva lot more funeral homes than I ever wanted to see. When my friend Linda died, I sat in the front, tears streaming down my face, even more aware of the fact that I couldn't wipe my own tears. It is so easy to let anger and frustration take over. Fortunately, my attendant Brian sat close by, wiping my tears, a reminder of the good in the world. But it's worse when I can't even go to the funeral home, which is the case since the Covid pandemic. Recently my dear friend Sharon passed away. While she was in the hospital, I couldn't visit. I called and talked to her in the ICU, and she gave every indication that she would be coming home. She spoke so positively about beating cancer. When I called Cindy to give her updates, I was positive too. Until the next time I had to call Cindy. I could hardly talk. "I can't believe I'm saying this because it's real when I say it out loud. We lost Sharon."

I can't help but feel sorrow when someone else has something bad happening in their life. It's like watching my accident from the outside, seeing the car on a trajectory and the boy running into it, with no way to stop the momentum of the action. There's the nagging sensation that things could be different if just one piece of the puzzle were altered, if we had left the house ten minutes later, if there had been a traffic jam, if the mailboxes had been on the other side of the road. But we can almost never stop the trajectory. We can only learn and try to do better in the future. The crazy thing is that now the mailboxes along that road are actually on the other side of the street. It's too late to save a little boy, too late to change my situation, but maybe it will save the next little boy and the next family.

Patience: The Virtue that Was Forced on Me

As I said, if I were given an official title, it would be Queen of Frustration and Queen of Patience—by necessity. I have to be patient, or I'd drive myself crazy. I don't let time spent waiting be idle time. You can do a lot of stuff in your mind with that waiting around time if you use it correctly. I concentrate on new ways to develop memory. Over the years I have improved my ability to meditate. I spend a lot of time waiting, praying, and preparing lists in my brain. When I see people, I ask them to write down my lists, though once I make them in my mind, I almost never forget them.

One time when I was volunteering at God's Kitchen, I needed to go downstairs to check on something. A colleague put me in the elevator and pushed the button, so I went down by myself. The plan was that somebody would meet me down there, but nobody came. I wheeled my chair around and checked on what I had come for. Then I waited. For a really long time. It was probably about twenty minutes, but definitely long enough that at one point I started wondering if anyone would ever come. I started thinking about what it would take to get myself out of there. I couldn't operate the phones they had at the time. I couldn't push a button on the elevator. It might have been easy to panic and feel trapped, abandoned. But I had to trust that somebody would come for me. My whole life is built on trust, on knowing what I can't do but trusting that someone else will help me, so I can do what I can do, and help others. Eventually, somebody came down in the elevator, spotted me, and said, "What are you doing?"

"I'm waiting for someone to come get me."

"You're a patient person."

"I'm the most patient person you've ever known," I said. "You have no idea."

If I had the secret of patience and could bottle it up, I would make a fortune. Or change the world. Of course, most of it comes down to having no choice, and recognizing that. I gave up the illusion of control. I could, of course, rage against my situation, and I have seen people do that. But they are often extremely unhappy, so that's their choice, but not a good one if you ask me. I have a lot to do, and my days are filled with commitments to the organizations and people I serve, so patience doesn't come from not having any demands on my time. And I would say that I, more than most people, have confronted the limited nature of life and the possibility of death, so patience doesn't come from feeling like I have an eternity to complete my mission in life.

Patience comes from a state of mind, an idea that the time I have is precious and I want to use every moment I can, either doing something or feeling peace, happiness, and love. When I have to wait, lists, prayers, and meditation suffuse me with those qualities, so I wait, and I use my thoughts as tools to achieve my goals.

Don't Be a
Complainer

*Not all of us can do great things. But we can do small
things with great love.*

— St. Teresa of Calcutta

When I first got out of the hospital, a nun
visited our apartment each week to serve as a
communion steward, allowing me to partake of
the sacrament as part of my congregation. At one point I
said to her, "If there's ever any volunteer work I could do on
the phone, like contacting potential volunteers, you let me
know." She came back the next week and said, "We're
looking for someone to make phone calls to schedule Meals
on Wheels for God's Kitchen. It would probably take one
hour a week. Currently, they only need volunteers three days
a week. The rest is covered by AmeriCorps." It was a start.

And truly, given how tired I felt, an hour or so a week making phone calls to schedule drivers was enough.

Mary K. and Brad Littell.

Recently, there has been a lot of research on the value of volunteering, in terms of the mental and physical health benefits for volunteers. I didn't have that research or need it back in the 1980s and '90s when I was recovering from my injuries. I simply needed something to do, and volunteering presented itself. I could do work that was meaningful and useful on my own terms without risk of losing the disability payments from my insurance that made it possible for me to live. By concentrating on something other than my disability, I developed coping skills. Plus, simply the need to budget my time to fit this volunteer work into my schedule made my days feel more productive. That built my self-esteem, which made me feel like I could take on even more.

I didn't want to spend all my time focused inward on my own situation and needs. When I looked outward, I could see a world full of needs, many that seemed more terrible than mine—or if not more terrible, equally difficult for the people who were suffering in different ways. No single person can fix all the ills of the world, but if each of us makes the choice to do what we can for one small part of the world, we can all lift each other up. As the Irish proverb says, "It is in the shelter of each other that people live."

God's Kitchen served two meals: one delivery of meals to seniors and others with challenges at noon (Meals on Wheels), and one in-house at about two-thirty in the afternoon. At eight a.m., cooks prepared the hot food. As a Catholic, I was proud to work at God's Kitchen because even though the organization was founded in our religion, we would help anyone who needed it without stipulations. People in need didn't have to answer questions, say prayers, or read scripture to be fed. It was meaningful work that made a real difference in people's lives.

For the people who couldn't come in for food, Meals on Wheels was a lifesaver. Acting as volunteer coordinator let me use the skills I had, and I could see a real difference in the lives of the recipients of the program, as well as the other volunteers. For some of the recipients, the food delivery each day was their only point of contact with another human being. We started deliveries at eleven in the morning and were done within two hours. I got volunteers by calling people and organizations I knew. I contacted churches and sometimes went to speak to groups. Most of the volunteers were retired people and seniors, and I enjoyed talking to them on the phone.

When I got new volunteers, I would meet them at God's Kitchen to get to know them and let them know about the position. Over 70% of the people we served were older women living on less than $7,000 a year. Even in the 1980s, that was barely anything. Meals on Wheels drivers had to understand that they were more than delivery drivers. They couldn't just leave the food on the doorsteps. For people who might not see anybody else during the day, having someone stop in to check on them was a huge comfort. I made sure the drivers knew they had to put eyes on every person they delivered to. Sadly, we had cases of people who passed away and the driver was the only person who noticed. I had each new driver ride along with an experienced volunteer until they were ready to deliver alone. Not only would drivers stop and talk to each person like a friend, sometimes they would take out the trash or shovel the driveway. Most of the people receiving meals needed help, but desperately needed human contact as well.

Within the year the person who was in charge of the program had a stroke. I gradually took over one route and then another, until eventually I handled them all. This was another turning point in my rehabilitation. I had fulfilling work to fill up most of my days. I set up two dozen routes with over 400 deliveries. For each route, I had to recruit about a dozen drivers to cover all the days, plus fill in when someone was out. I was grateful for my good memory, and I was forced to develop ways of remembering even more than I thought I could.

I worked from home because God's Kitchen didn't have the facilities I needed, but most mornings a group of volunteers gathered in the kitchen at God's Kitchen before opening and had coffee and donuts. Three women were the cooks, and they were always talking and laughing. Everybody loved being there, and I stopped by from time to time. Sometimes Jeff drove me there in the afternoon, and we pulled up to the building where a line of people waited for meals. I could roll along the line and say hi to them and talk for a few minutes. This was a place where people wanted to be because it was full of love.

Soon they asked me to produce the newsletter, followed by a place on the Advisory Committee, which meant more and more responsibilities, more and more challenges. I had to pace myself because I got tired, but the work was rewarding and it filled a hole in my life, in my soul. I ended up working almost forty hours a week as a volunteer, recruiting, planning, changing routes each day in response to people's changes in circumstance. My attendants helped on the computer or phone. But the most important skill I had to offer was in getting people involved. My friends joked that nobody ever said no to me, and that was a skill that came in handy. Humor and genuine concern went a long way. But the truth was that when your life depends on asking people to do things for you, asking becomes second nature. If I ever felt any reluctance to ask when I was younger, and I'm not sure I did, those feelings were totally gone. Asking is easy once you get used to it, and what's the worst that could happen? Somebody might say no. Then I moved on to the next person.

And in spite of my friends' teasing, people did say no to me. Frequently, I would call and leave a voicemail and never receive a call back. I'd send emails and get no response. Running into people at events was a great way to get to them. It does still surprise me when I get someone who says no. In truth, when I ask, I am actually offering the possibility to make a difference, to feel good about yourself, to do something meaningful. So even in the face of a million noes, I'll keep asking.

———

After volunteering for years and years, I got a new supervisor. Her name was Carol Greenburg, and she came in ready to make things happen. I was scheduled to go into the office for an interview with WOOD TV-8, our local news station, to speak about Meals on Wheels. I thought of the station as our guardian angel; whenever we needed something, they were there. I liked to keep the community informed about Meals on Wheels and the hidden needs that a lot of people would never encounter.

Good things really started to happen as Carol took over. Carol wrote grant proposals and found funding. We had a horrible basement for storage, and Carol was awarded grants to renovate it and get additional freezers and shelving. There was a wonky staircase that wasn't safe for anyone, and in addition to fixing that, we added a freight elevator to transport and store pallets of food. It made a world of difference.

Many of our guests who ate hot meals during the day let us know that when they went home, if they had homes, there was no food until the next day. We started a new program called Special Delivery, and I was the program director. At the time, a study conducted through Grand Valley State University confirmed that only about one-third of the people God's Kitchen was feeding at noontime had other sources of food. That meant that for about two-thirds of them, the meal we provided for lunch made up their total diet for the day. Delivering groceries was a way to make up that deficit. Many people, not understanding how God's Kitchen worked, donated small canned goods and other staples rather than the industrial sized containers we used to cook for hundreds of people. We used those donations for Special Delivery. We applied for and received a grant and also got food from Second Harvest Gleaners, which would become Feeding America. We put together grocery bags of food for the week and delivered them to households that might not be able to pick up food or might not have access to food in their neighborhoods. Carol secured more grants, and we ran the program with more volunteers.

Next, we realized that many of these people didn't have access to health services or mental health care. At that point I had my master's degree in social work, so I had the credentials to direct student interns, including nursing students from Grand Rapids Community College and social work and occupational therapy students from Grand Valley State University. I supervised the students on home visits to give medical and mental health assessments, make recommendations, and provide resources.

Sometimes when we had meetings, Carol would come to my home and sit by my bedside as I made calls and we talked and planned. By this time, I was working part-time, and she encouraged me to come on full-time and give up my disability status with Social Security.

"Let me think about it," I said. Of course, it felt wonderful that my hard work was recognized, but if I worked for a salary, I risked losing my disability payments. I would have to go into the facility more, though I could still do much of the work from home. With the high cost of medical care and everything else I needed, I was afraid that I had more to lose than I would gain. I couldn't jeopardize what was actually keeping me alive. Jeff and I talked, and we looked into our insurance policy and made calls to find out how working might affect me. In the end, I took the job. After eleven years of doing the work, I was hired!

———————

Master of Social Work: I Get my Face Slammed on Concrete

My sister Joanne died when she was 52 and I was 40. I was so angry at her for living a life that was unhealthy and stressful. I fought every day for life, and it felt like she just let hers slip away. With her help, I had made it through a long period of healing, and a lot of what I had was because of her dedicated work with insurance claims. I had had the opportunity to have a house full of teenagers and all the ups and downs that brought.

Her death was another moment of realization for me. *I'm not going to live forever*, I told myself. Anyone's life is too short, and I always felt that mine was precarious. In spite of my happy home life and success at God's Kitchen, I had lost a lot of my self-confidence. It occurred to me that if I gained some new skills, I might feel better about myself. I had considered getting a master's degree for a while, but I finally decided to go for it. I needed a new challenge, a way to stimulate my mind.

When I first proposed going back to work, the insurance company said they wouldn't pay to have an attendant accompany me on the job. They claimed my attendants would just be doing my work for me, so it would make more sense for any employer to just hire them. As a volunteer I didn't have to deal with that. Still, I wanted more for my life. I had been raised with the idea that I should be a leader and I had promised myself all those years before in the hospital that I would create a life that was meaningful.

Meaning is a shifting goal. What feels like a stretch and an accomplishment soon becomes commonplace. Even in the midst of life's most meaningful, rewarding and important activities, like parenting and being a loving spouse, family member, and friend, it is easy to lose a sense of self. Maybe it's especially true then. There is so much that calls us to focus on others rather than ourselves. In my case that was even more complicated because family members and friends often became my attendants, and attendants became like family. I was never just me, on my own.

With a master's degree, I would be recognized for my ability to think and strategize, something that an attendant couldn't do for me. In a group of people sitting around a table, I was just like everyone else. I had ideas and plans worth communicating and the ability to share my vision. This meant it would be me, just me, accomplishing what I needed to accomplish. This also meant the attendant could accompany me to work, to do things like drive me there, open doors, type what I dictated. But I was still considered the one who did the work.

This was 1992, when Mel was at Grand Rapids Community College, getting ready to move on to her four-year degree, and Stephanie was earning her teaching certificate. It seemed like the perfect time for me to go to school, too. Western Michigan University had a campus in Grand Rapids, and one of my cousins was a professor there in social work. I chose Western because it offered a degree in Policy, Planning and Administration (PPA). You could choose clinical or PPA, and policy was most intriguing to me. I didn't know that later my knowledge would help with forming Kids' Food Basket, but I knew it was all about finding a problem and meeting that need. Policy is boring, but changing or updating policy is interesting. Recalling my work as a lobbyist and how we dealt with ballot questions, government, and regulations was helpful. I knew there was more potential for burnout in social work, especially as a clinician working with certain populations like children and women suffering from domestic abuse. I had to decide where I might best be able to put my energy. Policy seemed the place for me.

My attendants drove me to class and took notes for me. Many of them were students themselves, so they were perfect for the work. I would read textbooks using adaptive equipment that held the books open and have my attendants turn the pages. I dictated my notes, and they wrote for me, so I could review them later. For exams, I would sit in the hall with my attendants, and they would write down my answers. I wrote papers by composing in my head and then dictating to attendants what to type. For group projects, I would meet with my group after class, discuss my contributions, and go home and have my attendants type up my part of the papers. There was a way to do everything I needed to do; I just had to work harder to find it.

My attendant Brad took me to a lot of my courses. As a student himself, he was already going to classes for culinary school. "Well, you get to learn extra for free now," I told him. One day after I had finished a paper for a class, we drove to the campus. I rolled onto the lift, and Brad hopped out of the van to open the door. On this particular day, the lift got stuck, and instead of being lowered, I rolled off it. My wheelchair and I fell three feet onto the concrete parking lot.

"Mary K.!" Brad yelled, astonishment and fear in his voice. He ran over to check on me and tried to lift the wheelchair. My seatbelt was caught. He partially lifted me again, but I was still stuck, and the wheelchair fell back down. Smack! My face slammed onto the concrete. Brad tried again anyway. Smack! My face slammed the concrete again. I started laughing.

"Brad, I'm belted in. You're slamming my face on the concrete," I cried through the laughter. What else could I do but laugh after finding myself in this crazy situation? Brad started laughing nervously with me. Soon we were full out laughing, me tipped over in my wheelchair caught in the seatbelt and Brad sitting on the asphalt next to me trying but failing to help. Some onlooker called an ambulance, and when the paramedics came over and attempted to lift me, they first tried to put a neck brace in place. I heard Brad say, "Don't worry, she's already paralyzed." We both started laughing again.

"Go hand in my paper and meet me at the hospital," I told him once I was in the ambulance. "Then call Jeff."

Once again, having no feeling in the lower part of my body meant it was impossible to tell if I was hurt or not. I had to go through an entire physical exam, but it turned out there were no major injuries. Jeff fixed the lift, and I went back to class the next week. The professor returned our papers, and I got an A.

"So, a bunch of you handed in papers late or asked for extensions," the prof said. "Look at Mary K. She was rushed to the hospital, but she still handed her paper in on time."

I had never wanted to be a teacher's pet, but it felt good. It had taken me until my graduate program to really understand what professors wanted, what it meant to learn, to investigate and understand how the world worked. Now I was an adult and wasn't screwing off like an undergrad. I was much more interested in what professors were talking about, especially the diversity classes and abnormal psych. All of it felt germane to what I was going to do. I was also already working in my field and knew that in my heart I was always meant to be a social worker. In my coursework, I had many chances to plug volunteer management into coursework. For a nonprofit, volunteers are essential to the work. No organization could survive without understanding how to recruit them, train them, make them part of the team, and reward them. I wanted to be the best at that, and I could see how my education could build on my experience.

More importantly, I was ready to move onto a new phase in my life. I didn't know for sure all that would be involved, but I knew the more I did, the more I would be prepared for whatever might come my way. The course of my life was determined by having been at the wrong place at the wrong time. Moving forward, I would try to be at the right place at the right time.

————

Public Speaking: Try Not to Sound Like an Idiot

I was prepared for public speaking from my first job working for a lobbyist in Lansing and my second job coordinating the State for a ballot question. I was frequently interviewed by the press and gave speeches. Before I was injured, I often spoke on television in front of a large viewing audience. But after my accident I lost confidence in myself for many years. With my disability, if I went to a place and they wanted me to speak, it might be difficult to get up on a stage because of accessibility issues, and they always ended up fumbling around with the microphone to get it to my level. My voice was not strong because of my respiratory issues. I had more things to deal with than before the car accident. It was difficult to see myself as the same person with all that had changed. Speaking to large groups of people or being interviewed by newscasters took a lot of energy, and for a long time, I didn't have that energy. I had to give myself pep talks. I knew deep down I could do it, and I knew my message was important, so I would tell myself I might as well do a good job at it. Jeff would help me rehearse my speeches and attend when I had a speaking engagement. Afterwards, I would ask him, "How many umms were there?" He would encourage me, "Not many. You were great."

I started doing public speaking as a volunteer, then employee, at God's Kitchen. I was interviewed frequently by local news media where I tried to inform the public about our programs. I took any opportunity for good public relations. I wanted to spread the word in a way that would inspire people to act.

And to try to be a little funny.

I was invited to speak at the Mount Mercy Alumni Association breakfast, which was held every Christmas. I rolled into the room and there sat my old principal and my senior class political science teacher who had become president of ADAC Plastics—not all the teachers were nuns. I gasped when I saw the crowd. I hadn't taken it seriously enough, which was appropriate given my high school experiences. I actually wrote the speech I would give during breakfast. I started with, "I'm living proof that a solid C student can make something of life if they work hard enough." That started my talk with a laugh. The rest felt easy.

Another time, I was invited to speak at the International

Women's Leaders Conference at Amway Corporation. Once again, I didn't have a speech prepared. I have to admit, I was feeling vulnerable and uncertain as I wheeled myself up on the stage. There was no way I would let myself give in to those fears. I just started to speak from my heart. I don't remember what I said, but by the end, I was crying and most of the audience was crying. The power of sharing our stories, of connecting on a human level no matter what our circumstances, cannot be overrated.

A nearby town had a program for a community book reading, emceed by a writer. They were discussing JoJo Mayes' book, *Me Before You*. I was asked to present. The emcee asked if I had read the book, and I hadn't, but I told her I would. By the time I presented at the event, I had read the book and was able to comment on the main character's life and his choices. It was about a guy who was a quadriplegic who sought assisted suicide. The book did a good job of describing what it was like to live as a quadriplegic, but, otherwise, I told the moderator I couldn't relate to the story. I told her, "Every day, everything I do is a fight to stay alive."

"Well, talk about that, then," she told me. I went to the auditorium in the local high school, where audience members asked me questions about the accident and my early years of rehabilitation. They asked questions about Kids' Food Basket.

Jeff was up there with me. Someone asked, "How do you maintain your sanity in day-to-day life?" Jeff jumped in. He had thought about it, too, having lived with the tragedy for much of his life, though in different ways.

He said, "If the mind is idle, then it has a lot of time to wallow in the bad things. If you are busy and looking forward to the future, life can have so much meaning. Otherwise, life is just day to day, paycheck to paycheck. That's true for anybody, disabled or not."

My answer was the same: "I stay sane by being busy and productive."

Surprisingly, what helped me feel better about public speaking was watching television. I'd see the news and watch the way some people they interviewed spoke. I would tell myself, "I couldn't sound as dumb as these idiots, so I'll be okay." That was all the pep talk I needed.

My job now at Kids' Food Basket involves a lot of talking, something I am entirely equipped to do. I recruit volunteers and donors. I go to schools and talk to the kids who design fundraisers to benefit Kids' Food Basket. I attend luncheons and fundraisers and meetings of organizations, and I spread the word about children who live with food insecurity and our work to nourish them. My best advice for speaking is to be honest and speak from the heart. I also consider the situation and the audience and try to say something meaningful to them.

The truth is, though, that the work I am doing was so important that I just can't let myself get in the way. Thinking too much about how people look at me or if I sound stupid would stop me from relating to the people I need to reach. I've never been hungry, but I've known more loss and pain than I ever thought possible. I have served clients who are homeless, poor, in chronic pain, living with disabilities, lonely, or experiencing hunger. I know what it is like to be on the fringe, unnoticed, or worse, noticed by people who gawk and feel superior. I know what it is to wonder if I can help myself, if I can count on anybody else to help me. I know the hopelessness of feeling like things will never change. But I also know the hope of making things change. I know that each and every human being born on this earth deserves to live a life of hope, a life free from hunger, a life of dignity. With only my voice and my knowledge, I have enough to speak out and try to make things happen.

A Lick and a Promise

Americans are really good at acute compassion, but pretty bad at chronic empathy. We, without question, haul strangers out of a raging flood, give blood, give food, give shelter. But we are lousy at legislating safe, sustainable communities, at eldercare, at accessible streets and buildings. It is the long-term work that makes disasters less damaging. But we don't want to give to the needy, we want to save the endangered. We don't like being care workers, we want to be heroes. The world does not need more heroes. We need more care."

— SIGRID ELLIS

When I went back to school for my master's degree, I had a different view of the world than I had when I was younger. Having been part of the disenfranchised and having faced so many situations where I was on the fringe, I had a better understanding of not only the disabled community, but of what it is like for everyone who is on the outside looking in. I don't know if that made me more receptive when I met MaryAnn Prisichenko and learned about the need to feed kids who were losing out on educational opportunities because they were experiencing hunger. Truth be told, I can't imagine not having access to food. What I discovered along the way is that feeding kids is not rocket science, but the situation is very complex when you get down to the reasons for food insecurity in childhood and what we are going to do about it.

Mary K. and MaryAnn Prisichenko with kids from Sibley Elementary.

Sometimes I wonder how I can live in a place that would let kids and families struggle for the barest necessities, like nourishing food. It feels like such an obvious thing to be against. Then I remember that I don't live in that place. In such a place, Kids' Food Basket wouldn't exist. There wouldn't be thousands of volunteers and donors and employees and board members who decided that feeding kids would be a priority. Of course, I know we are just one small place in a big world with lots of problems, but I keep thinking it's a start. I think the people who don't support these efforts probably don't understand the problem. They see a simple solution: make their parents responsible for feeding them. But there are no simple solutions in a world of complex systems and long-held beliefs. It takes effort to understand the economic and social systems that are in place that make hunger endemic in a world of plenty. I wasn't thinking about any of that at the time. Kids' Food Basket evolved into an organization that works to address these issues much later. Just like that commercial from the 1980s, "Time to Make the Donuts," my only thought was, "Time to feed those kids."

As volunteers at God's Kitchen were packaging the boxes for drivers to pick up for Meals on Wheels or Special Delivery, I would wheel around the warehouse to check on supplies and talk to volunteers. One of them mentioned that she was heading over to a local elementary school when we finished for the day. She planned to bring juice boxes and granola bars for the kids there. I knew of the school, Straight Elementary, and that it was located in a very poor part of town. She told me the story of the school's principal. Her name was MaryAnn Prisichenko, and she was trying to find ways to give her students the same opportunities and resources that kids from more affluent neighborhoods had. A big one was food. Some of them had only potato chips or cookies for dinner. Some had nothing at all.

When she told me about kids who went home from school and had no food there, I was appalled. What kind of parents wouldn't even give their kids food at night? My first thought was that we should report the parents for neglect. Like a lot of people, I thought the parents should take full responsibility for feeding their kids. It didn't occur to me, and I learned later, that many of the students lived in two-parent households where both parents had minimum wage jobs, and couldn't afford rent, heat, transportation, *and* food. Many of these families lived in homes that weren't insulated and drove cars in constant need of repairs. They faced high gasoline, utilities, rent, and food prices and had to make tough decisions. The conditions they lived in were stressful.

Of course, I should have realized there was a problem. After all, I was feeding adults who lacked food every day. It stood to reason that some of them must have families, and that meant kids who needed nourishing food. Plus, people in that area lived in what used to be called a food desert, what we now call "food apartheid" because it focuses on the social and economic causes of the phenomenon. When an area gets too poor, grocery stores move out. Residents have almost no access to the kind of shopping the rest of us take for granted. They often have to drive long distances to get to the grocery store in an unreliable vehicle, using valuable resources like gas and time. The result is geographic segregation and systematic denial of resources. Often the only accessible source to buy food might be a gas station, where snacks and drinks are the only options. If parents were providing potato chips for dinner, it was because that was the best they could do. *But someone should be able to do better*, I thought.

So, I got a phone number and called MaryAnn to talk to her about the situation. I planned to meet her at Straight Elementary, but my regular attendant wasn't available. Jeff drove me over, and we parked in the lot behind the school then wheeled around to the front entrance, where we talked into an intercom to gain entrance. We went through a set of double glass doors and into the main office of the elementary school.

"Oh no, I got sent to the principal's office again," I joked with Jeff as we waited.

"Wouldn't be the first time, would it?" he said.

MaryAnn came to meet us and brought us back to her office. She was very persuasive. She had been looking for help for a couple of months. She had exhausted every church, food pantry, and nonprofit she could think of. I couldn't imagine that so many people could ignore this problem once they knew about it. Still, I wasn't sure what I could do, so I didn't make any promises.

She started by telling us that she was a brand new principal and had taught for fifteen years. She had been sent to Straight Elementary because it was a struggling school.

"When I first got here," she said, "I walked into the school and immediately saw there was no library and no playground because the original equipment was unsafe. The school board chose to have it pulled out, and there hasn't been money to replace it."

I agreed that was sad, but I knew that wasn't why I was there.

"People don't realize the number of things that are stopping kids from being successful beyond just reading and math scores. But I thought, 'I got this.' I went to the radio station WSNX and fundraised for the playground. Two of their DJs funded it through their foundation, Steve & Sabrina's Kids. The Peter Wege foundation donated funds for the library," MaryAnn explained.

"Sounds like you have a lot of support in the community," I said.

"Yes, but let me tell you what happened, and you'll see why I feel like this is more than I can fix. Kids who experience hunger have difficulties learning, and most of the time, they can never unlearn that. They can never unlearn that the world is difficult and adults will let you down. I don't want any kid to have to live with that, and I certainly don't want the kids at my school to feel that way."

I wanted to say something, but I started imagining those kids, so I waited, and MaryAnn continued.

"I went into the cafeteria during lunchtime. There was a little girl from a low-income family, and she was wearing an oversized yellow calico dress. She was digging through the trash cans outside the cafeteria, and I saw her putting food in her huge pockets. I didn't want to scare her, but I needed to know what was happening, so I asked as kindly as I could, 'What are you doing?' Her answer was, 'We don't have food at home, so I'm taking food for my family.' All I can tell you is that I went back to my office and sobbed for this six-year-old girl. I knew I could fix those other things, but this was bigger than me."

"What about the lunch program? Can't they send food home with kids?"

"Food service program regulations from the FDA say you aren't allowed to send food home with kids for all kinds of reasons that make no sense to me. I've tried them, and I've tried several other organizations. So far, nobody says they can help. We have after school programs for some of the kids, and they get food there, but it's mostly things like a toaster pastry and a chocolate milk. My friend saw me sobbing over it, so she started to come over to my house in the mornings and we make extra lunches for these kids, but I just keep finding more and more kids in need, and I know we need a solution that's bigger than us." At this point, MaryAnn was tearing up.

Food insecurity is something no kid should have to endure in a country like America that has so much abundance. I had known what she was going to tell me when I came in, but hearing the story from MaryAnn made the situation even more real. I started thinking about Mel, happy and healthy, and how much it hurt when she suffered. I couldn't imagine being a parent, especially a parent who was trying, and having my kid up at night with hunger pangs. I couldn't imagine being a kid, scared and hungry, not knowing if there was going to be any food until the next time I got a school lunch. It was heartbreaking.

"I'll see what I can do," I said. "I have been looking for a mission, and this is it."

"Thank you, Mary K. I can tell by the look in your eye

that you're serious. That means a lot. Now I can focus on the problems I can solve."

As Jeff and I went back to the van, all I could say was, "Wow, this is so damn sad." I guess deep down I was aware that childhood hunger existed, but it felt like a slap in the face to see it firsthand just miles from where I grew up in such a happy childhood.

———————

After the meeting, we drove through the neighborhoods surrounding the elementary school to get back on the highway. Of course, I knew about this neighborhood and knew there were a lot of low-income families. From MaryAnn, I had found out that people here were the poorest of the poor in our city. The percentage of kids who received free and reduced lunch was 98%—that's a lot of kids with parents who have struggles. There was a nutritionist at Second Harvest Gleaners who was working on her master's thesis, studying the important difference between feeding children a meal of empty calories versus a meal with protein and other nutrients from whole grains, fruits, and vegetables. Of course, it's easy to assume a healthy diet would make a difference, but seeing the *data* on that difference was impactful. I kept picturing kids sitting in one of these rundown houses, eating junk food, or possibly nothing at all.

Since we were both involved in feeding the hungry when we worked together at God's Kitchen, Carol Greenwood and I often shared information. She had given me an article about a nonprofit in California that was serving dinner to kids. A woman had learned that kids had breakfast and lunch at school but had no program to feed them during the summer. According to the article, she got an old ice cream truck, drove around the neighborhoods with the music playing, and when kids came out, she gave them free sandwiches instead of ice cream. I remembered thinking at the time how sad it was for those kids in Los Angeles. Now I was seeing it in my own city of Grand Rapids. I didn't know at the time how important that article would be.

The next day, I went to Catholic Human Development Outreach (CHDO). I had been serving as a sort of interim director of God's Kitchen because Carol had left for a new position in hospice care, but I knew I wouldn't have the resources to tackle this problem on my own. I told a fairly new director about the kids at Straight Elementary, but she, on behalf of Catholic Human Development Outreach, said no.

Because of the climate in 2001 after the bombings in New York City and the Pentagon and the unstable environment in the financial world, people were cutting programs. Nobody was starting new programs. Immediately after 9/11 there was a feeling of solidarity among Americans. An outpouring of charitable giving was sparked by the tragedy that affected so many families. Of course, most of that money went to support the victims of the World Trade Center bombings. Shortly after that, we experienced rising polarity. Anger was directed not only at the perpetrators, but at each other, as different factions of the country had different reactions to the prospect of war. Financial markets went crazy, and the damage rippled through the economy and throughout the world. Many families faced uncertainty, and charitable giving in general went down. There was more need, but less money to meet that need. We had felt it at God's Kitchen, and I wasn't surprised at the response I got.

I also wasn't willing to give up.

I went home, still thinking about those kids. I latched onto that thought and couldn't let it go. That night, I tried to sleep, but couldn't. I kept thinking about children not eating, innocent children not having food, children digging through garbage to get something to eat. Those thoughts did not sit well with me.

When I got to work the next day, I called the director at CHDO to talk again. "You said money was the problem. If I can raise money and get volunteers, can I do it? I'll start with kids at three schools. MaryAnn has identified 25 students at Straight, 50 at Sibley and 50 at Harrison Park who need help. I'm sure I can find enough for these 125 kids."

She was quiet on the other end of the line, clearly weighing my proposal. Finally she spoke, "I'll have to let you know." A day later she called and said yes. It was going to be a no-name program, funded by any money I could raise, with God's Kitchen acting as fiduciary for donations. I knew how to get food, get volunteers, and get the sack suppers to the schools. I would draw on all my experience and connections. The whole concept of Kids' Food Basket was as simple as it was revolutionary: kids had a right to the food they needed to flourish, so their community would provide it in the form of sack suppers delivered to their schools, which they could take home for a healthy dinner that required no preparation. That meant the brown paper bags we used to take our lunches to school as kids would go home with kids and they would have a sandwich, drink, fruit, and a snack.

So, I structured my days. I would get to work at God's Kitchen and the volunteers would come in the morning to put together the hot meal that we would send out for Meals on Wheels. At the same time, other volunteers would be packing up the groceries that would be delivered to people's homes. I did my job getting over two dozen drivers on the routes I set up for efficient delivery to people all over Grand Rapids and the surrounding areas of Wyoming, Kentwood, and Comstock Park. Then a new set of volunteers would come in to make the meal we would serve at noon.

I thought to myself, "Now, I have another program to work on." The solution seemed obvious. First, I had to find some money. When I was fifteen years old, my brother Terry took me to a Christmas party thrown by his then-girlfriend's family. It was thrilling to go to the event, and I met the people who would soon become his in-laws, Armen and Patricia Oumedian. They had established a family foundation and were well-known and generous philanthropists.

It's interesting to note that I could have felt a distance from them as the in-laws of my older brother, but instead I grew to love and become friends with them, Armen especially. Life worked out that way, but it made me aware that there are all kinds of people who we meet who we could become close to, but life and circumstances or our own reticence stop us. I try to make sure that never happens. Armen was a kind and fun-loving man, who was easy to talk to. After my injury, he would make sure to talk to me at any family events. He knew of my work at God's Kitchen and supported it with donations. He and Pat also volunteered, along with Terry and Pam and their kids. As I was working out the details for Kids' Food Basket, he was the first person who came to mind. I called him, hoping for a little help. He gave me $1,000. And then another $1,000. But even more than that, he became my mentor, someone I could bounce ideas off, and someone with experience who would give me advice in the kindest way.

One of the other volunteers, Mary Plaggemars, also donated $1,000. I was able to get food that was donated to God's Kitchen but wasn't being used for meals or Special Delivery there, and that included bread, and at first peanut butter, until we went peanut free due to allergies. God's Kitchen also let me use their account with Second Harvest Gleaners. We got 70% to 80% of our food from them at deeply discounted prices. I made up the menus for meals I thought kids would like, the same kind of meals I would have enjoyed as a child. We made sure there was a piece of fruit. It wasn't until later that I thought of vegetables because apparently I really was thinking like a kid. We would get granola bars or those little packets of cheese and crackers. That first $3,000 lasted through the entire school year, making 150 sack dinners five days a week, with money left over to start up again in the fall.

Then I had to work out the logistics. Between the time Meals on Wheels went out but before the lunch service, I would have a new set of volunteers come in. Maybe I couldn't make sandwiches or put a piece of fruit in a sack, but I could get the food we needed, and I could find people to volunteer. I could figure out the logistics for delivery. I had them set up an assembly line, with some people making sandwiches and others putting everything in a brown paper bag: sandwich, banana, granola bar, juice box. In no time, it seemed, we would have 150 lunches ready to go out. I set up two routes for drivers, one that went to Sibley and Straight Elementary Schools, since they were right near each other, and another that went to Harrison Park. Sometimes the drivers were volunteers, sometimes I had my interns go, and sometimes Jeff drove. If it worked out, some of the lunch assembly line volunteers just took the sack suppers and delivered them as they returned to work or home.

MaryAnn had told me that it was important to have consistency in delivering the sack suppers. Kids needed a sense of stability, a confidence that they would not have to be afraid of being without food again. When they went to a food pantry with their families, if they did, they never knew what they would get, and most of it was food they couldn't prepare themselves anyway. In the classroom or after school programs, they got food that was more like a snack or a treat, rather than a meal.

My imagination kept pulling me back to how frightening it must be for a kid who did not know where dinner was coming from—like a dagger in my heart. I thought about my own childhood, about how I and all the kids I knew took for granted going home to dinner after a day of playing hide and seek or riding bikes. I thought about Mel, and how we had tried to give her a sense of stability—and even more than that, a sense of love and togetherness. I wanted these meals to convey a sense of connection and love to the children who got them, a confidence that the community around them cared about them and would rise to the challenge of feeding them, no matter what their circumstances at home. Because one thing was for damn sure: Kids were not responsible for the circumstances they were born into.

And it's true that many of these kids come from homes with parents who are drug addicts or imprisoned. They come from homes where parents are neglectful or abusive. Sometimes they live with grandparents or in foster homes. Often they come from families that just can't make enough to cover living expenses, even with two parents working. Whatever the situation, it is not the kids' fault and the only hope of sending them on a different path is to feed and nurture them in ways they might not get at home. Whatever kind of home they come from, if they're undernourished, we feed them.

In May, just before the end of that first school year of feeding kids, I got a new job offer. I had been at God's Kitchen as a volunteer and then an employee for 22 years and I had earned a master's degree. Doing this kind of meaningful work, helping others, had been my way of saving myself. One of the regular volunteers approached me. He ran the Center for Independent Living, which would become Disability Advocates. He wanted to hire me. It felt good to have someone recognize the work I had done. My friend Carol had left the year before, and I was ready for a change. This new challenge would allow me to help people like me, the people who were ignored, whose regular difficulties were so often magnified by a world that didn't meet their needs. It was an opportunity I couldn't pass up, even though I loved the work I did at God's Kitchen.

Then I thought about my little pack of volunteers making and delivering sack suppers to schools. I thought about those kids. Could I trust this program to God's Kitchen when they weren't even sure they wanted it in the beginning? What would happen if there weren't funds available? The program didn't even have a name, and I knew it was something so important that I couldn't let it drop, no matter where I went.

I wrote my letter of resignation.

God's Kitchen had hired a new director when I resigned in 2002. I gave her the letter that basically said, "I'm resigning and taking the kids' meal program with me."

She said, "You can't. That's our program."

I said, "I can and I am—I've done everything to keep that program running. I'm not sure it will continue to exist without me. There are lots of kids who are experiencing hunger and you should find some we aren't serving if you want to help kids." Surprisingly, she did just that. She made a commitment to serve kids at two other elementaries. I had loved and appreciated my work at God's Kitchen and the people I worked with there. It wasn't easy to go, but I felt an absolute certainty about taking that program with me.

I found a local church that would let us use the basement. I still was able to get food from Second Harvest Gleaners. I still had my volunteers. For the last two months of the school year, as I was working at Disability Advocates, I had volunteers putting sack dinners together and delivering them every day. In the evenings when I got home from work, I would make phone calls and coordinate the next day's meals and deliveries until the end of the school year. I had the summer to figure out how to manage all of this along with my new job at Disability Advocates. I spent my days working on programs to help educate businesses, community organizations, and families about accessibility and resources for people with disabilities and my nights planning for the next year. There was money left from the seed money I had gotten. I knew there would have to be a nonprofit entity if I was going to be able to collect more donations.

Around that time I attended a Ferguson Hospital open house, and ran into George Heartwell, who was a professor at Aquinas College in its Community Leadership program and who would become mayor of Grand Rapids. I knew George from a variety of committees that we both served on in our shared goal of serving our community. I told him what I was working on. "George, I need an intern who can help me manage this," I said. I had worked with interns at God's Kitchen in the Special Delivery Program I had instituted, so I knew one dedicated intern was all I would need to keep things going. George didn't even need to think about it.

"I have just the intern for you. This works out well because I have been looking for something worthwhile that would be a challenge and learning experience for her," he said. The next week Bridget Clark called me. Even as a college student, besides being willing to do the work, Bridget understood the basic steps needed to set up a 501-3c. She knew some people who could serve on a board of directors. I had some people in mind as well. Bridget found a lawyer who filed the paperwork, and one of my trusted volunteers was a CPA who was willing to help on the financial end. A strong program needs a good leader, but the leader's job is to find enthusiastic, willing people and put systems in place. Then the program can take off. I had always been good at connecting with people, with finding what their passions were and how to make the most of them.

Once the board was set up, we realized that if I couldn't be present, we needed someone who could answer questions for anyone making inquiries who might want to volunteer or donate. The board decided to give Bridget the title of Executive Director and Intern. She would have the authority to field questions and help manage the systems I set up for volunteers making and delivering meals. This was the beginning of our year-round service and the foundation for all the organization accomplished over the years (See Appendix 1).

Use Your Strength for Others

Love recognizes no barriers. It jumps hurdles, leaps fences,
penetrates walls to arrive at its destination full of hope.

— Maya Angelou

I had been working with people who couldn't just run to the grocery store to stock up or pop into a local restaurant when the cupboards were bare. Households experiencing food insecurity hover around 10% nationwide. Of course, this level of poverty tends to affect people of color, people with disabilities, and the LGBTQ+ community disproportionately. But hunger falls more heavily on children with about 20% living day to day without having enough food. That's because in a household there may be only one adult with many children. And at crucial areas of development, lack of nourishing food can mean long-term physical and intellectual losses. Even if you don't embrace feeding kids for kids' sake, the cost of not doing so is high in terms of increased health care costs, increased incarceration, lower economic potential, increased school dropouts. We had been gathering data about food insecurity from a variety of sources, but recently, Michigan Governor Whitmer created the Food Security Council, and their report is informative (See Appendix 2).

Mary K. with volunteers at KFB: (L to R) Deb Anderson, Melissa Shea, Tim O'Brien, Gregg Robinson.

I used some of our previously acquired data when George Heartwell took us to meet with the Dyer Ives Foundation where we requested funding. We needed to pay Bridget for the extra hours each week she worked beyond her internship. After our presentation, Dyer Ives awarded us $10,000 for her first year. I was feeling pretty good about the plan I had put together, but then one of the trustees said,

"Mary K., if it was anyone else, I don't think we would give this money."

As we left, I turned to George and said, "I guess my business plan wasn't as good as I thought. Maybe it's the letters after my name. Thank goodness I have my master's degree. These people like letters after your name."

"You found a need in the community, and you came up with a way to fill it. That's what's important," George said.

I have always said that our mission is something that is easy to wrap your arms around, to wrap your heart around. Feeding kids experiencing hunger—there's no downside to that. It's something every community should do.

But every story has an adversary, and ours came in the form of a food service employee. It's hard to imagine why, but my guess is there was a perceived threat, an implication that food service wasn't doing its job if students went home undernourished. Why the hell this person didn't just try to help us and show that these accusations were wrong, I'll never know. Instead, this particular food service employee, charged with nourishing kids, tried to stop us from feeding them when they were away from school and would have been going to sleep with stomachs growling from hunger.

I was shocked when a health department employee contacted me to say that a complaint had been filed against us. After all my time working at God's Kitchen—and with several of the volunteers from God's Kitchen doing double duty helping us—I was sure we were following all precautions for food preparation. But the complaint was that since we delivered to the schools during the day, and the kids didn't eat the sack suppers until later that night, the food sat without refrigeration for too long and would spoil. This sounded insane to me because if a person at the school really believed that, why not provide a tiny space in the refrigerators at school to store the meals until the kids could take them home? Most kids who bring their own meals to school put their lunchboxes in their lockers for half the day before eating them, and nobody sees a problem with that.

Nevertheless, the health department inspector came to investigate. There wasn't much to spoil in our little sack suppers. We were still using peanut butter and jelly for sandwiches and so far, nobody had told us that any kid who was receiving the meals was allergic. Once we got refrigeration, we changed that, just to be cautious. When the health inspector cleared us, there was a collective sigh of relief. I couldn't believe that anyone would object to feeding kids, but I had worked with enough bureaucrats to have been worried. Eventually, the food service worker came around and supported our mission. Once I had seen those kids who so appreciated their sack suppers, I couldn't imagine stopping.

It's tempting when even the small challenges start to add up, to say, "This is too hard." Or, "I don't know how to do this." I had spent so much of my life facing hard things, things I never imagined I would face when I was a young woman. Is it possible that I became so used to adversity that I just looked at another obstacle and without thinking rolled over it, crushing it like the grass under my wheels? I'm not sure why I couldn't let difficulties stop me, but I think looking at them as a problem with a solution I just had to find, rather than a roadblock that would stop me, was invaluable.

———

We continued to build our board, adding interesting, accomplished people as board members. Some we pulled from volunteers. There was Mark Cebula, a weekend volunteer, who had helped with fundraising at God's Kitchen. We also asked Louise Kempker, a secretary of God's Kitchen. Then there was a wonderful man named Joe Crump, who Bridget brought on board. Bridget also had a friend who was a grant writer for Grand Valley State University, Steven DePolo.

As a board, we developed bylaws and somehow put everything together. We needed a name. I went online and read about an organization called Children's Food Basket. There are no new ideas, and I liked the idea of "basket." Obviously, I couldn't use a name already taken. Plus, it was a little more formal than I wanted. There was something about the idea of letting kids be kids that stuck with me. We filed under "Kids' Food Basket." Then we continued to build awareness. One of our board members, Kyle Caldwell, was with the Michigan Campus Compact and he felt Bridget qualified to earn money as an intern, so Bridget wrote a grant and received more funding.

Another of our board members knew the owner of the DeltaPlex and he lent Kids' Food Basket space in an old factory down on Monroe that he also owned. There's a pattern in my life; I meet a lot of people, and I'm never shy about asking them to help. People love to help when given the chance, especially if you ask for something specific they are capable of doing. The truth is, I'd rather ask someone to donate something for free to help a cause than sell anything to anybody any day. Selling something is giving value for value. Asking for a donation or for people to volunteer is giving someone the opportunity to receive endless value, meaning, and purpose for a small price.

I used to think that power was working to earn the respect of coworkers. I learned that power actually means getting what you need with the least number of calls at the lowest cost. My goal was one call and free. But I would make more calls if I had to.

As Kids' Food Basket grew, we became strategic on board development. Before anyone can become a board member, they have to serve as a volunteer for six months. As soon as a new board member begins, we hold an orientation where we invite them to join a committee and discuss our different programs and present policies and procedures. We also hold a board retreat to talk about strategic planning. And just for fun, we have beer and wine at our board meetings.

As we built our board, we knew we needed an expert in nutrition, and someone knowledgeable about fundraising. Bridget's dad and brother are lawyers, and we invited people from banks, too. John Arnold, one of the first board members, was director of Second Harvest Gleaners, now Feeding America, dedicated to providing access to low-cost, healthy food. Along with a great board and Bridget's hard work, we grew because we stuck with my vision of being community oriented and flexible. We started having volunteers make sack suppers on evenings and weekends. We stored them and delivered them the next day. Bridget managed the whole thing. She not only understood the business aspect of our mission, she was focused on the kids. She had the brilliant idea to have volunteers decorate the brown paper bags with pictures and inspiring messages for the kids who received them. It's amazing how much kids prize those bags and love those words of inspiration.

———

When I resigned from God's Kitchen and learned that its new director was going to supply meals for two more schools, I had wondered how she thought she was going to fund the additional meals. By the next August, I was informed that she was leaving God's Kitchen. Her supervisor told me, "She's made a verbal contract to feed kids, 50 at each school. Otherwise, they will be without food at home. Can you take them on?" Of course, we did. We weren't planning to expand, but there was no way I was going to leave 100 kids who were expecting meals every day without food. I wasn't sure how Bridget and I, along with our volunteers, were going to handle that extra commitment. Today, Kids' Food Basket has very well-defined steps to adding new schools, and once we make a commitment, we will never go to a school and tell them we don't have the funds to feed their kids.

The thing is, when you say you don't want kids to suffer, it's impossible to choose some kids to feed and others to not feed. Obviously, I knew there were kids all over the community and all over the state, country, and world who were food insecure. And obviously we didn't have the resources to help them all. Still, I was committed to doing whatever I could whenever I could.

I thought of a quote often attributed to John Wesley: "Do all the good you can, by all the means you can, in all the ways you can, in all the places you can, at all the times you can, to all the people you can, as long as ever you can." That fit well with my own mantra: focus on what I *can* do. We would have to find a way. That might be one of our early mistakes and something we learned from. Growth is sometimes seen as inevitable, but that doesn't mean you can't manage it effectively. Over time, we would grow and learn how to make sure we were prepared for all the demands we wanted to meet. At that time, I thought adding two more schools would involve a lot of running around for Bridget.

I met a guy who was director of the Salvation Army after school program, which was located near the two new schools. We had volunteers there make and pack sack suppers, which meant we had volunteers working from two different sites. It turned out that rather than saving work, having volunteers in two separate spots added work. We stuck it out for a year, but over the next summer, when we continued feeding kids even if they weren't in school, we regrouped.

By the end of the first pilot year, we were making the original 150 sack suppers plus the two new schools for a total of 250. Volunteers came in evenings and then on Sundays. We had facilitators, wonderful people from Thor-

WHAT I CAN DO

napple Evangelical Church, and Bob Kingma from King-ma's Market, to help coordinate.

We outgrew our donated space and found a larger space with an office. Once we moved to our new space, Bob Kingma said, "Kids' Food Basket needs a commercial refrigerator." I went to meet with him and asked, "How much?" The answer was daunting: $150,000. Bob reached out to the refrigeration people he bought from, and they got workers to donate time and used parts to make us a walk-in cooler. Now we could make the whole sack supper, load the carts, and roll them right into the cooler each day. When drivers came, we just rolled out the carts and put the sack suppers into cars—no more fear of complaints from meddling food service employees.

Over time, we also started hiring more staff. With more kids to feed; more volunteers to recruit, train, and manage; more community and school outreach; more donations and inventory to manage; more of everything, it became clear that Bridget and I couldn't handle it all. I retired from Disability Advocates, partly because of health reasons and partly so I could dedicate myself to Kids' Food Basket. I took on the role of advisor and Bridget, after graduating college, took on a full-time position as Executive Director. Our staff is made up of talented, dedicated people, and their links to the community are important to us, which means we have people from diverse backgrounds serving kids from diverse backgrounds.

————

Whenever I could, I would stop in and meet with Bridget and visit on weekends or evenings to thank people. At first I felt, "Wow, we are doing a wonderful thing." But growth was challenging, and the need was so great. At board meetings, we discussed how we could get more money or find food at a better cost. We tried to figure out how we were going to keep up our momentum and keep feeding all those kids.

Anything that is worthwhile is not easy. You always encounter stumbling blocks and pitfalls. But just like I wouldn't give up when I was in the hospital faced with no choice but to find a life after my injuries, just like I wouldn't give up in rehab, I decided I would have no choice but to figure this out. But I didn't have to do it alone. I prefer to work as a team member, and I was part of a great team. Bridget is a great leader and our board members, along with the small staff we had at the time, jumped in feet first so we could address growth issues.

With our tagline, "We're dedicated to stopping childhood hunger," we weren't going to stop at 250 kids. Still, we didn't say, "We know of 5,000 kids, let's feed them." I worked with Bridget and the board to achieve calculated growth. We developed a matrix for decision making to determine when we could take on new schools. We asked questions: How willing are they to work with us? Who do they serve? What age are their kids? Early on we didn't feed anyone over twelve years old. Younger kids were a higher risk. It wasn't that we didn't care about older kids, but we couldn't overextend ourselves because then we would fail everybody. Our main target early on was Grand Rapids

Public Schools, where at least 80% or more of the students receive free or reduced-cost breakfast and lunch. We lowered it to 70% as resources increased. After the pandemic, we expanded to help entire families who were food insecure. We collaborated with Meijer, and they sent food to kids and families over the weekend from their grocery stores.

We did a lot of things to test how to best serve our mission. Some of them went well, and some of them didn't. But there are several things we did that I think are noteworthy. First, we made it possible for everyone to be involved. Food insecurity is a community issue as well as a statewide and national issue. Whether you are a person who is in a situation of food insecurity, or you are a person who is part of the economic system where some of us benefit from the labor of those who can't afford food even while working, you are involved in this issue.

Kids' Food Basket makes it possible for anyone to be part of the solution, which is why we made sure anyone who wanted to could volunteer. If this was a community organization, then the community should be part of it. Just like I had found purpose in my life through volunteer work, I wanted to extend that opportunity to anyone who needed it. About 78% of the families who benefit from sack suppers have had a chance to volunteer at Kids' Food Basket. We have a fantastic emphasis on kids helping kids, and about 33% of our volunteers are under 18. We allow volunteers as young as five years old to contribute to our mission. A volunteer could also be 95 and sit at home and color bags while watching *The Price is Right* and be part of the solution.

We get volunteers not only from churches, but from Boy and Girl Scouts, school PTAs, nursing homes, and group homes. We have about 36 groups of people with disabilities who volunteer. There are over 30 clubs and organizations just from Grand Valley State University whose members volunteer regularly to support us. Our board and staff are wonderful, and Bridget has done an amazing job of growing the organization and its mission, but I say to anybody who will listen that the volunteers are the heart of Kids' Food Basket, the reason we can do what we do.

We make it as convenient as possible to volunteer. For instance, we have volunteers schedule their times online, so they can control when they work and choose the job they want to do. We accept groups, such as businesses, clubs, or schools. Our staff does the best job of thanking people for volunteering. If we have a business that regularly sends a group, we send thank you boards and thank you videos. Bridget had the idea for the thank you boards, which are decorated with photos and notes from kids who received meals. Whenever I go into a business and see a giant board that says, "We support Kids' Food Basket," my heart wells up with gratitude. We send donors and volunteers thank you notes written by kids who received the sack suppers the volunteers packed. We have a Volunteer Appreciation Day at the end of the school year. There is a week set aside in April where any volunteer can stop by our facility for popcorn and t-shirts. I stop in all the time and talk to the volunteers to get to know them and thank them.

———

Kids' Food Basket is "a movement that seeks to meet immediate nutritional needs while planting the seeds of sustainable change for generations to come." The core belief of the organization is that food is a right for every person. In our economic system there is an underlying assumption that you only deserve what you need if you can pay for it. But that attitude fails to recognize that every person on this earth has value, not for what they can produce or do for others, but for the fact of their existence. If there is anything I believe in, it is in the inherent value of life, and every day I have lived that truth. If life has value, it supersedes any systems created by humans that say money is more important.

It's an organization about food, so we also have the right people involved. We have a nutritionist who studies the role of good nutrition in childhood development and helps plan out the meals. Each day, we provide at least 1,000 calories of a well-balanced meal that kids or families don't have to do anything to prepare, so even the kindergarteners are assured of nourishment. Kids' calorie needs for growth range from 1200 to 1800 calories, so we know the meal we provide has to be a big contributing factor to their growth. We have received testimonials from schools about kids suddenly being able to concentrate in school, with better learning and better behavior, simply because they are not experiencing hunger.

Local chefs have taken an interest in Kids' Food Basket, too. They were especially interested in our work because they had concerns about the quality of the snacks kids were getting at school—it wasn't real food, just a snack, and often it wasn't healthy. Every year, we have a fundraiser called Feast for Kids. All the food is donated by local chefs. All the chefs who contribute are winners from the Chef's Association's best of the year. It's a mixed message, because we raise money and awareness for kids who experience hunger, but at Feast for Kids, guests eat the best meal of their lives. But that's the nature of fundraising.

We also involve the kids who receive the meals. Not only can they and their families volunteer, but each year we collect information from them. Their teachers or someone from Kids' Food Basket surveys children about what they like and don't like in their meals. We make sure to limit waste. First question: opt in or opt out? If you have food that kids aren't eating, how do you get it out of their bag and into a box to give to someone else?

Through our surveys, we find out how they feel about the meals being delivered and how we can provide the meals and still show respect for their privacy. In the beginning, each teacher in the schools we served was challenged with finding a way to give a sack supper to the kids so they wouldn't feel singled out and stigmatized. They would put it in their lockers, signal the kids, have them in a back corner of the room, so kids grab as they go out. Of course, in schools where everyone needed food, they were not stigmatized. Our teams work with a point person at each school to give ideas of how other schools handle distribution.

Our staff visits schools regularly and are often greeted by throngs of enthusiastic kids. I love it because I know they are learning so much, especially that the community supports them, and that compassion is important. I know for sure that both Mel and JJ have grown into people with a deep sense of compassion because they have seen my struggles and triumphs. I share that with other kids as I speak to their schools and classrooms.

Kids are excited and interested. They share thoughts and ask questions. One year, a little girl raised her hand after my talk. She told me that her sister had to do a project on a notable American, which involved writing a biography and dressing up as the person. Her sister had chosen me. I remembered her sister. She had called me, and I told her everything she needed to know. Another school does a fundraiser every year. We talk to them, and they decide what they want to do. We told them how some groups have pickle sales to raise money. They decided to do that. Some schools also have an assignment to write to area businesses and inform them about Kids' Food Basket. When Wolverine Worldwide donated $10,000, a kid phoned me. He was so excited because he had sent his letter to them, and he thought he was responsible for getting the donation. It means so much for kids to believe they can make things happen.

It helps that we have a very compelling, easy to understand mission. It's a powerful feeling when you are putting that sandwich in the bag knowing that if you weren't doing that a kid wouldn't eat. It's a task that's doable; there are hurdles, but you can jump over them. Initially we had trouble when we expanded to Muskegon, where many live at the poverty level. When we started, we met with the United Way and Muskegon Foundation, and they were very helpful. They gave us people, money, and advice. They made sure we served one school in the Heights; otherwise, they said we wouldn't get old time donors. It's where all the problems are, so if we didn't provide meals there, it would be hard to build awareness and people wouldn't be as supportive. To serve the community in this important way, you have to become part of the community, you have to know what its needs are and how to work with people to meet those needs.

We've also had accusations of white savior complex. All I can say is that MaryAnn went to dozens of organizations in the community looking for someone to help her feed her students, and none of them responded—White, Black, Hispanic, whatever. I didn't respond because I was White. I responded because I couldn't let kids suffer when I had the resources to help. I responded because those kids were part of my community, no matter what their ethnic background. I responded because I knew what it was like to see others enjoy the comforts of society when you are sitting on the sidelines watching, and I didn't want those kids to feel that way. At least in this one area, I could make sure they knew they had a right to healthy food that nourished their bodies, a right to go to school and learn, a right to the prospect of a better life. Because all life is precious and where there is life, there is hope.

———

We began to receive testimonials from schools. They were starting to meet adequate yearly progress goals, and they thought it was because their kids were finally being nourished. There are so many factors that help kids improve, and it's difficult to sort out just one cause, but definitely being nourished has a big impact. Slowly and then with increasing momentum, the stories started to roll in from teachers, staff, and volunteers. Surveys conducted by Kids' Food Basket found that 100% of educator participants reported that Sack Suppers were either somewhat or very helpful in improving students' social-emotional well-being. Similarly, 70% reported Sack Suppers as somewhat or very helpful for improvement in behavior and 80% reported them to be somewhat or very helpful for improvement of academic performance. Providing nourishing meals and breaking down barriers of access, affordability, and education helps children be their fullest, best selves.

One day, when I was still at God's Kitchen and coordinating the sack suppers, a volunteer found me in a room by myself, crying.

"What happened?" she asked me.

"I was talking to a school administrator. She told me about a little girl who got her first sack supper on the first day after Christmas break, having switched to her school midway though the year. The next day, she returned to school, and she still had part of the sandwich and snack in her lunch bag. Her teacher asked her, 'What's wrong? Didn't you like the food?'

"'I'm saving it for today, because I know I won't have dinner again,' the girl told her.

"'Oh, sweetie, we're going to give you another meal today,' The little girl couldn't believe it."

"It's so hard to imagine a little girl getting so excited about something we all take for granted," the volunteer said.

"It's the kind of stuff that gives you pause, but also makes you more determined. I want to make sure she understands that we have her back," I said. We both cried together for a moment, then we got back to work.

And we heard other stories. A teacher at Sibley Elementary passed out sack suppers as kids were getting ready to leave school. She noticed she was one bag short. The next day, she paid extra attention and saw a little girl taking two. She was a girl who started school after the winter break, and she had been identified as being at risk. When Mary asked why she was taking two suppers, the girl explained that she had a three-year-old sister at home who she was responsible for after school. The extra meal was so she could feed her, too. After that, we changed our policy so that if a child had younger siblings who weren't in school, we would give them extra meals to take home.

Another time, a teacher brought a young boy who received sack suppers to a board meeting as part of a group of students to talk about what was best for them. When a board member asked what he liked and didn't like in his meals, he got vague, which could have been shyness, but we weren't sure. The teacher thought it was strange, so the next day she watched as he went outdoors after school and cut across the courtyard. Two bigger boys caught up with him, and she thought the boys were going to bully him and take his food. But the little boy walked right over to those boys, laid out his sack supper, and each picked what they wanted.

It turns out he was sharing food with his brother and older cousin.

One volunteer task we have children and other volunteers do is color the brown paper bags with pictures and words of inspiration. We learned of a teacher who went on a home visit to one of her students. The seven-year-old shyly showed the teacher his room. On the wall next to his bunk, he had hung the bags that his sack suppers had come home in. Bag after bag lined the walls like wallpaper. Each inspirational message, each lovingly crafted drawing. The teacher asked him, "Why do you keep those?" He answered, "Because they are mine." I thought about the cards that had hung on the walls of my hospital room in the ICU all those years ago and the bank envelopes with Jeff's loving messages, which I had saved and cherished throughout the years.

We heard over and over how kids would get so excited to read those messages and pictures on their bags. They would share and talk to each other about what they got. Those bags are a symbol for what a community can do, and when she came to perform a concert, Lady Gaga even decorated a bag.

They're not only good for the recipients, but those bags are inspirational to the people who create them, too. As I said before, we want to make sure that people who don't have the means can still be part of our mission, to find a way that everyone can be part of the solution. Kids make bags for other kids. Girl and Boy Scout troops decorate bags and even prisoners volunteer to decorate bags with inspiring messages for the kids. There was a newspaper article about an older woman who reached the milestone of decorating 10,000 bags. She said it gave her a reason to get up in the morning.

MaryAnn called me about an adult care facility where residents volunteered to deliver food and told me, "Thursdays are my favorite day because every Thursday we are reminded how important everyone is to this mission. We know the serenity prayer, we all know it takes a village, we all know the give a fish story, but we don't live it every day."

MaryAnn had been stopping in and we had been in touch during the building of Kids' Food Basket, but she was happy to leave the work to me with all the other problems she was solving at the school. Then one day she called me and said, "You know how those meals go home? Well, one of our students asked for extra sack suppers for the family. If it weren't for that, we wouldn't have found that they were all homeless, living in a car." She was crying. The sack supper that was meant for home wasn't going home because home was a car. MaryAnn and her team were able to find a shelter and eventually a home for them. If it weren't for the sack supper, we might have never even known. MaryAnn asked me, "We keep saying, 'Sack supper going home.' How many times did they go to a car because of homelessness? Most of the time, kids aren't willing to disclose these traumatic events in their family, but this time one did because the whole family needed food."

We started in borrowed space in a church basement, moved to more borrowed space in a former factory, then to one rented space, then another. Now Kids' Food Basket has moved to our own facility. We do not only feed kids, we advocate for change, educate our community, and have added a Kids' Food Basket farm so kids can learn about growing fresh fruits and vegetables. But mostly, we make sack suppers that feed thousands of kids who otherwise might experience hunger.

I feel like I started rolling up a giant ball of yarn from a tiny strand, and it just keeps growing. We keep finding new needs, new ways to address those needs and new understanding about how the systems in our society create the issues of hunger and poverty, and how we have to adapt to keep feeding kids. Each generation ties a new string onto the last and starts building up this giant ball with their own colors. This became so true to me when a young girl who had received meals when she was in elementary school, grew up, started her own business, and became a board member at Kids' Food Basket. She had started in poverty, with a mother who was a drug addict, leaving her and her sisters alone and neglected, then moved into foster care and adoption. All those safeguards in our community worked together to save her, and many more in similar situations. And now, she is passing it on. I wish I could live long enough to see how big it's going to be.

Learn from Life

The days, months, and years eventually reveal, like a Polaroid, a clear picture of how significant events and decisions ultimately shape our lives.

— HODA KOTB

This book was written during the Covid-19 pandemic, and during a time of strife in our country and our world. But then again, isn't it always a time of strife, at least for some people, somewhere? That doesn't mean there isn't room for hope. We just have to find it within ourselves. I'm a person who is especially vulnerable to illness and I've spent more time in doctors' offices and hospitals than I want to tally. My spinal cord injury means my respiratory system is compromised, so a disease that might mean shortness of breath for some people could mean death for me. I'm also one of the people who might be seen as on the fringe of society because of my disability. So many choose their own convenience over consideration of the safety of others, which means that with raging infections out in the world, I had to stay in.

At the White House in 2010 with Mary K., her niece Stephanie Tomaszek, and Bridget Clark Whitney.

When we first suspected there might be a pandemic, Jeff and I were in the Florida Keys. We planned to continue on to Hutchinson Island on the Atlantic side of the state. As we were traveling from Islamorada, people were saying the situation was getting bad, and everyone should go home. I was just recovering from pneumonia and Jeff had been sick. We cut our trip short. When we got home, Jeff and I were alone, except for Mel and JJ. They stayed at their house but since they weren't out in public (Mel worked from home and JJ's school was virtual) they were able to come over to visit sometimes. Mostly, we didn't leave the house, except when Jeff went to Meijer for groceries. I didn't go out of the house at all for over six weeks during the winter of 2020. For a person as active as I am, that was a challenge. People have some idea that those of us with disabilities don't need to go anywhere or do anything. That is absolutely not true. In addition to feeling trapped at home, we had to manage without the attendants I rely on to keep my life going. Mel helped with a lot around the house that attendants might normally do when she was visiting, but most of the work fell to Jeff. The situation was difficult for us all.

I felt a lot of frustration—and I already operate at a pretty high level of frustrating situations—and a sense of being trapped. I already have to ask others for everything. I already have to face the mountain of things I can't do. There's no doubt the pandemic exacerbated this. It took an effort to remind myself that I had no choice, or really two choices: 1) be miserable or 2) figure out the things I could do and find a way to live. Those were the same two choices I had faced since I was 27. Now everybody had those choices. I got the sense that a lot of people had never faced such a crossroads. I told myself, "I gotta entertain myself, so what am I going to do? I can bellyache that I'm trapped, or I can catch up on reading, watch movies, plant a garden, order in food I want. Make the best of it. That's what I always do."

JJ often said, "This is the most boring day ever."

"You think you're bored? Imagine how I feel. I can't do anything. You have to find something to do. If you're bored, it's because you are boring. Let's play a game."

We were lucky. I knew a lot of people who were totally on their own. Under the best of circumstances, I can't be alone. But I also think that if you don't have people around you to quarantine with, it's not good for mental stability. Once again, I was thankful for the relationships that sustain me and for the phone that kept us in touch with all those people.

Given the pandemic and the turmoil in our citizenry and government, it would have been easy to let external things throw me off balance, to not think as logically or not drum up the coping skills I needed. In regular life we get so much thrown at us at one time, it's like we're all on overload anyway, and then there's a pandemic thrown in. I spoke with my very wise 93-year-old father-in-law about all the negative forces we seemed to be facing.

"How do you get through all that, George?"

"I dismiss it from my mind." Pearls of wisdom come from different moments. Someone says something at the right time, and I pause and internalize it. Sometimes it's the consistent exposure to another person and their way of handling the bullshit that I learn from. I tell myself that we all have trials in life, and "If they can weather the storm, so can I."

When the pandemic hit, a portion of our Kids' Food Basket staff had underlying medical conditions, so they had to work remotely. They could still do anything that had to be done on a computer, like reaching out to donors or writing newsletters, but the physical work of preparing meals was a challenge. Staff members who were able bodied had to pick up the slack. Many schools couldn't have volunteers at their sites, and when schools shut down, we realized how vulnerable our children were. They didn't have the haven of school or the care of teachers and others for food, for intellectual and mental health support, for physical activity. Many families who were food insecure sunk deeper and had almost no access to food when their schools and workplaces shut down. The United Way had a helpline and people in need could call 211. At the beginning of the pandemic, if someone called and said, "I'm here with my family and we don't have food," they didn't have a solution. All the pantries were closed.

Within 48 hours, someone called us and said they couldn't get help from the United Way. The staff at Kids' Food Basket realized the problem and came up with a solution. Those distraught 211 calls would be directed to us and staff members who could be physically present in the warehouse packed boxes of food and delivered them. We were as innovative as we could be to get food to a new point B in place of schools.

We partnered with other organizations and made alliances with them. We partnered with a number of churches, like Catherine's Care at St. Alphonsus, where kids could easily pick up sack suppers, and we worked with schools that had personnel on site to distribute food, too. We worked with Mel Trotter, an organization that helps the homeless and those experiencing hunger. Seeing all the diverse groups working together to better understand and alleviate childhood hunger and the ramifications to families was inspiring. With all that was going wrong, I had to focus on what we could do that was right. I was so very proud of the innovation and the way the staff regrouped to rise to the occasion.

In the past, we had to deal with difficulties, situations like dips in donations, which meant thinner sandwiches or a little less food than usual, and even crazy weather. The year before the pandemic, Michigan had so many snow days due to the Polar Vortex there were some days that we didn't know how we were going to get the sack suppers to the kids. The amazing staff at Kids' Food Basket figured out that since city buses were still running, they could take the food to bus stops and families who didn't have food could pick it up there. Staff with four-wheel drive vehicles actually delivered food to families when the roads were too covered with snow and ice for most people to travel.

At a board meeting, Bridget reported that a staff member stopped and picked up extra groceries for a family in need. I knew right away that she was talking about Brad, my former attendant. Every one of these stories fills me with pride. I said my story was a love story, and there are just so many ways to experience love. The pandemic was just one more way we had to find innovative ways to continue to support our community. We get better at adapting every time we face a new challenge if we focus on our goals and the people we care about.

———————

Nobody does this work for the awards, but I'm not going to lie, I love a good party. Awards ceremonies are usually good parties. I had received awards before I started Kids' Food Basket, including the "Unsung Hero Award" from WOOD-TV8 (but once I got the award, doesn't that mean I was sung?), the "Friend to the Physically Challenged Award" from Ambucs, and the YWCA "Tribute Award" for my work at God's Kitchen. One of my favorites is the "Honorary Black Belt" from Western Michigan Tae Kwon Do Association. I like to think that if I had the use of my arms and legs, Jeff and I might have practiced martial arts together, and maybe I would have earned a black belt. It's a nice dream, but I have to put it aside right away and get on with my reality.

My work at Kids' Food Basket means we are invited to fundraising events and awards ceremonies all over the city and the United States. People will say, "Let's have lunch." I've met many famous and impressive people, including President Barack Obama, Diane Keaton, Julianne Moore, Michigan Governors Snyder and Granholm, and Hoda Kotb. That makes up a good part of our social calendar.

I've been named as one of the "50 Most Influential Women in West Michigan" and, most recently, one of MLIVE's "10 Women Who Shaped Michigan." Among others, I have been a recipient of the Art Van "Hope Award," "Invest in Ability Award," and the "Grimod de la Reyniere Award" from the Greater Grand Rapids Chefs' Association. I've been a "Points of Light" recipient and I've been a recipient of the state of Michigan "Governor George Romney Lifetime Achievement Award" from Governor

Snyder. Every award is meaningful to me not only because I appreciate the recognition for my work, but because each one represents the triumph of hope over adversity.

And, as I said, I like a good celebration. At the end of 2014 when I was awarded the "L'Oreal of Paris Women of Worth Award," we planned to combine it with a celebration of my 60th birthday. We had wanted to celebrate when I actually turned 60, but I got sick at the time and couldn't travel. For the L'Oreal awards, we went to New York City and stayed near Times Square. Jeff, Mel, Stephanie and I had a great time. I hadn't been to New York City in years.

When we got to the awards ceremony, I leaned over to Stephanie and said, "I think there may be some movie stars here." We met Julianne Moore, Eva Longoria, Blake Lively, Andie McDowell. Hoda Kotb was my sponsor and sat next to me at our table and introduced me at the ceremony. I told her, "I'm so glad you are the one who is introducing me." She is so positive and engaging. I was so happy when she said to me, "I wanted to introduce you, too."

Diane Keaton sat at our table, as well. During the meal, she leaned over to me and nodded toward Jeff.

"Who is this?" she asked.

"My husband."

"He's easy on the eyes," she said. Jeff will be living off that forever.

———

I felt both honored and humbled by the attention, and even when I wanted to shy away from it, I would remember that I would have a bigger audience to talk about Kids' Food Basket and the important work we were doing. Any award ceremony or newspaper article was a chance to bring the issue of childhood food insecurity to the public in a vast arena. But nothing compared to the award I received in 2010. I had been told that Bridget nominated me, but I wasn't really thinking about it. Then I received the letter. I told Jeff and Mel and we cheered. Then I called Stephanie.

"Hey, remember that award I was nominated for? I got it."

"Okay," she said. She sounded like she wasn't paying attention. I don't think she remembered any award or knew what I was talking about.

"Well, I can see you're unimpressed. Let me read you my acceptance letter," I said. She laughed. I'm sure she could tell I was teasing her. "It says, 'The President of the United States is looking forward to meeting you.'" That got her attention. I laughed. I was overjoyed.

"Oh, my gosh." That was all she could muster to say.

"Yeah, you want to come with me?"

Then I called Carol, who was working at Spectrum Health Continuing Care in a program for people with spinal cord injuries.

"I'm going to Washington, D.C.," I said.

"What? When?"

"Well, I have to be there in time for my awards ceremony for the Presidential Citizens Medal." I could hear a commotion as Carol jumped out of her chair, she cheered, and her assistant ran into the office.

"Mary K. is getting the Presidential Citizens Medal," I

heard her explain to her assistant. "I want to go!" she said to me.

"You can come. I'm allowed to bring guests."

"Yes, but me? That's such an honor."

It was an honor I wanted to share, so in the end, Jeff, Stephanie, Brad, and Carol came with us. Bridget flew down and met us, but the rest of us took a road trip in the van. Our plan was to drive to D.C., stay one night in the hotel, attend the ceremony, then drive home. The awards committee was covering the cost of transportation and one night in the hotel, but staying longer would have been really expensive. We would stay for the reception after the awards, which was lovely, then head home.

We all had to have security clearance from the White House. Stephanie took me to the dress rehearsal. We pulled up to the address we had been given, which was just a block away from where we were staying. A guy walked over to the van and seemed to know immediately who we were.

"Stephanie Tomaszek? Pull over here," he told us. We headed in the direction he indicated.

"How do I pull over to a wall?" Stephanie asked me. I couldn't see much, but it looked like there was a wall that formed a barricade right where he told us to go. Fortunately, someone else walked over and gave us directions to pull up to a set of pillars and then drive down into the underground parking.

Once we got there, we had to pull up to a canine unit.

"Stephanie Kathleen, do not talk to that dog," I warned her. I knew how she felt about animals, and she could spend ten minutes petting any dog we passed. It felt like we were never going to get to the dress rehearsal.

"I was going to tell him he works for the president and he's doing a good job."

"I'm sure he already knows."

Stephanie did my hair and makeup. I wore a beautiful lace blouse with a blue jacket. I had a purple and black rose on my lapel, just for a little flourish. I love flowers and purple is my favorite color. It was ninety degrees in Washington, D.C. and it took a while waiting in line to go through security to get into the White House, but I felt giddy and excited. We all did.

I was ushered into a room with the other recipients, and we talked together for about an hour. Then we went to our seats.

It turns out that the event was taking place on Barack Obama's 49th birthday. He walked in with a big smile, and we all stood up and sang "Happy Birthday." He presented the stories of all the awardees, and it was interesting to hear what they had done. I felt honored to be in such company. When it was my turn, Jeff went up with me, to accept the medal on my behalf.

President Obama leaned to face me directly in my wheel-chair and whispered, "Thank you for doing what you do."

————

Doing what I do seemed like the only choice I had, not only for the kids, but for myself. I had listened to those lessons of my parents and found a way to become the leader they wanted me to be and, more importantly, to serve my community. I had fulfilled the promise I made to myself in my hospital bed to build and maintain important relationships and to build a life full of purpose and happiness. Doing what I do had saved my life. Doing what I do had saved so many children in ways I never imagined when I started.

There are days, even weeks and months, when I don't want to think about my paralysis, about my life and having to give instructions to sustain it. But then I start tallying the positive just like I always do: loving husband, great family, wonderful friends, meaningful work, and JJ, who now serves as my reality check. He'll say things to me like, "Grandma you can't do that because you're paralyzed." And I tell him that with enough will, I will find another way. I have a full life because I knew how important it was to develop coping skills, focus on others, and do something extraordinary so I could feel better about myself. I have physical limitations, but my brain is still intact. I can come up with a plan, and I can make sure that plan comes to fruition, so something positive happens. Not everybody has those skills, but everyone has some talents that can be developed if they are willing to work for something important.

When I said my life was a love story, I meant it. But no love story is simple. My life hasn't been the kind of love story you see in movies where there's a misunderstanding or argument that is easily resolved. My love story is a story of finding a way to embrace life. It is using my voice to help advocate for people on the margins. It is love as an act, not love as a feeling. And more than that, it is love as constant action.

———

"I'm having a hard time as a student understanding what you go through every day. Can you explain it in a way everybody could understand?" a student asked. Jeff and I were at a seminar at Grand Valley State University giving a talk about my experiences. One of the students who had come to Kids' Food Basket to do a report on us had invited me, saying she would get extra credit in her graduate level social work class if she invited a guest speaker. The professor asked if I could come to speak to undergraduate classes, too. I pulled my wheelchair up to a table at the front and Jeff sat next to me. The professor was behind a podium fielding questions from the bright, ambitious students.

"I can answer that," Jeff said, knowing how trying it was for me to explain. "That's the easiest question in world. This is how I've explained it to hundreds of people. Do you have a favorite chair in your house? Do you have any duct tape? What if someone came over to your house tonight and put you in your favorite chair then duct taped your feet and your hands, your waist and chest to the chair. You wouldn't be able to do anything for yourself. Over the next 24 hours, anything you need, you have to ask someone for. If your nose itches, ask. If a hair falls across your eyes, ask. If your throat is dry and you need a sip of water, ask. Bodily functions? Ask. And remember that sometimes you will have to wait until someone notices or has the time to respond."

Jeff's explanation is pretty accurate. There are times when my life is incredibly frustrating, and I feel totally vulnerable. I get used to it for a while and then I get tired of it again. I felt like I adjusted to it for the first five or six years because it was the only way I could survive, and then it was frustrating again when my sister Joanne died. My emotions and my ability to deal with my life ebb and flow. There are times when I feel confident about my ability to maintain my sanity and other times it's not as easy.

The students in the classroom were quiet after Jeff's answer. I didn't think I had anything to add, so I let the silence sink in. It's tiring to explain my life all the time. We tend to avoid discomfort in social situations, but there are times when it makes sense to feel discomfort. Those moments are opportunities to develop empathy, to feel sorrow, to allow the motivation for action to blossom.

At the end of our presentation to the class, a student raised her hand. "I don't have a question. I have a comment. You restored my faith in men," she said to Jeff. I thought about all those years ago, the doctors at Craig Hospital telling me that men are more likely to leave than women. Maybe it's just certain men, maybe it's that nobody has faith in them, and they have no help or support. Maybe it's just that we have lower expectations for men as caretakers than for women. People rise to expectations. That's a source of hope for all of us.

So here I am, busy and engaged, having overcome tragedy and built a pretty happy life, given my disability. I still say paralysis sucks, but it doesn't make life impossible. I've definitely learned a lot along the way. I would have been a damned fool if I had not because life is a journey of experiences and learning lessons. Sometimes we succeed and sometimes we fail. The best we can hope for is to learn from our experiences and be more enlightened and more progressive as we age.

Recently one of my former attendants called me. She was in tears, because she was going through a hard time, maybe had been going through a hard time since she was young because she didn't have a great family life. I listened. I was thinking about people who have issues from childhood. You have one life, so you can rehash all that, or you can do the best you can with what you have. I told her what I thought: "Life is screwed up, and when it comes right down to it, we really can only depend on ourselves. I know it's hard."

That sounds crazy coming from me because I depend on everybody for everything. I would be nowhere fast without my help. All of my life's work has been about helping others, founded on the belief that as human beings we all deserve to be the recipients and givers of care. That belief is what compelled me to start Kids' Food Basket and to take it to a church basement with a handful of volunteers. What I was trying to tell her was even with all the help and support that anyone can get, what happens in life still seems to come down to what is happening in your own mind. My life is proof that even when you can't control what happens to you, you can control how you think about it and where you focus your energy. There is always hope if you can learn resilience and find your own strengths. The people who love and support you can't give you the will to create a meaningful life—they can't even tell you what your meaningful life should be. You have to rely on yourself and on your ability to keep trying even when you feel down.

You have to believe that you are worth it, that life is worth it.

A lot of mental health comes down to having a purpose. I'm mentally better with more activity, more challenges; that's when my self-esteem is high. I had to retire due to health, but I have been active on many boards and with my work at Kids' Food Basket where I focus on public relations and fund development. When there isn't stuff to do, my mind wanders. I think things like, "What the hell am I doing here anyway?" When I start those thoughts, it's easy to get caught up in them and harder to find the energy to do something so that I can rise from the well of despair.

I'm a firm believer in therapy, too, though not all therapists are equal. You have to find one who meshes with you. I find simply having to verbalize my fears, issues, and stumbling blocks helps me organize my thoughts and think through my situation better. Having a good therapist, though, helps even more.

And we all need to be recharged, by going to dinner with friends, visiting the zoo with a grandchild, or reading a good book. The best remedy is to call up a friend, a person who listens to your troubles then gets you laughing and joking. It's a relief to talk to them about the challenges. And, of course, I always have Jeff. I can't think of anything that has been more important in my life than to have a spouse I can count on.

My father-in-law once told me, "Peace comes from within." I really did a lot of soul searching and intellectualizing about what those simple words meant. How do I incorporate that wisdom into my life, into daily rituals that help me keep peace, internalize peace, radiate peace? Deep breathing helps me regroup. And always, I return to prayer and meditation.

Rituals and my spiritual beliefs have become an important part of my life. I still pray each morning the first thing when I awake. I pray it's a good day, pray loved ones will stay safe, pray we have enough volunteers for Kids' Food Basket to keep feeding children, and a litany of prayers for special people around me. Prayers and meditation have allowed me to create peace in my mind. They are a time of contemplation, a time that renews me to take action, a time to consider what actions I need to take. We are all part physical and part mental. When the physical isn't cooperating, it is important to work on your mental stamina. Developing strong coping skills is important.

Prayer and meditation help because shaping your inner life (and your outer life for that matter) comes down to mind over matter. "Mind over matter" is such an easy sounding cliche. The truth is that conquering my mind was anything but easy. First, I had to recognize that negative thoughts, thoughts about my past, what I lost, even about my present circumstances, would only hurt me. When I had those thoughts, I had to take notice, and tell myself, "Stop." Then I forced my mind in a new direction, thinking about something, anything, positive. I would let my mind dwell on the people I love, the next fun thing I would be doing, the work I do.

———

I had a friend who used to send me notes of encouragement all the time. When I was still in rehab, she gave me a book about Joni Eareckson, a woman injured in a diving accident. She was trying to tell me, "This isn't the end of your life." Lots of people have to regroup. She was trying to show me that my life would be what I wanted it to be, if I used my mind to make things happen.

Although I'd never say I am grateful for my injuries or wish this on anyone else, I can say that I have learned a lot, that I have been spurred on by trying to overcome my challenges, and that I feel like I have had a positive effect on the people around me. When I look at Mel or JJ, I realize that their knowledge that I'm disabled and their knowing I haven't let it deter me from other things has been a positive influence in their lives. They are more open to seeing how other people live and how other people navigate life. I think I have shown them that resilience is the most important characteristic, and that it comes from a love of life, from hope.

As I am helping raise my six-year-old grandson, I want to show him all this without breaking him. He's strong willed and easily frustrated. And soon, he will be physically bigger than me, and, of course, he's already stronger and more able bodied. I often have to discipline him from bed. It takes a lot of patience. I'll tell him, "You listen to me." As much as a six-year-old can, he listens. Just like when Mel was young, I have to be respectful of my role. I'm part of a team, not taking over raising him myself. But I have definite ideas about what kind of person he should be in the world, and I want to teach him what I have learned: I want to teach him about love and compassion, about the power of hope, about the way he can make decisions about his life, and I want him to know that the way he thinks about his circumstances will shape him. I want to protect him from anything bad, but knowing that is impossible, I want him to be able to find the strength within himself to face and overcome—and to focus on the good. To find hope and to cling to it like the life preserver it is.

And I want to teach him to live a life full of laughter. Be able to laugh at yourself, laugh at everything around you. Don't take yourself too seriously. Even when you need to have a good cry and good laugh at the same time, laughter is key. Enjoying life and finding humor everywhere is so important.

Love, joy, laughter, purpose: those are the gifts that make a life worth living. Life is sustained by the hope that any of these might be found in the next moment. They are the gifts I gave to myself when I decided to live a life focused not on what I lost, but on what I have, on what I can do.

ACKNOWLEDGMENTS

There are so many people to thank because a book doesn't come into being without a lot of help. First of all, we have to thank MaryAnn Prisichenko for getting the whole thing started. As the principal who saw a little girl searching for food, she set a chain reaction in motion that allowed Mary K. to start a movement that has changed the lives of so many children. And for that little girl in the yellow calico dress who had the courage to tell the truth about her situation, so a solution could be found, we have so much respect and gratitude. But MaryAnn is also responsible for the book itself. She brought Lisa and Mary K. together, and she applied her considerable persuasive talents to convince Mary K. that telling her story would inspire people and serve as a way to offer hope at a time when hope is crucial. Plus, she's a really good friend.

We also have to thank George Heartwell for enthusiastically writing the introduction to this book. Also, many people participated in interviews with Lisa to provide material for her to incorporate into the book, and we want to thank them for their time and honesty, including Jeff Hoodhood, Mel Hoodhood, Stephanie Tomaszek Deindorfer, Mike Roach, Terry Roach, Cindy Williams, Maria

Corstange, Brad Littell, MaryAnn Prisichenko, and Carol Greenburg.

When the book was in draft form, we had beta readers give us feedback, including Jodi Nikolagic, Lori Dunn, Stephanie Tomaszek Deindorfer, Judy Ball, and Catherine Creamer. But we are especially grateful to Lisa's husband David Rein, who read the book thoroughly and offered developmental editing feedback. He also provided the financial support that allowed Lisa to take the time off other projects to write the book without worries. Deb Bek Moore read the book multiple times to serve as copy editor, using her extensive knowledge of the English language and made the book so much better in the process. We can't thank her enough.

Mary K.'s attendants pitched in to help make this book possible in many ways from helping Mary K. read drafts and make suggestions to giving enthusiastic support. Julie Riedy helped with technology and Melissa Shea read the book with Mary K. But as the book makes clear, Mary K.'s attendants make everything in her life possible, and she wants to thank them for all the work they do.

Mary K. would like to thank John and Amanda Wheeler for their continuous support of her and everything she does. She would also like to thank the people at Walker AMBUCS for their monetary support: LouAnne and Steve Davis, Lisa and Steve Monroe, Rachel Nicks and Michael Larsen, Cheryl Phillips Lemieux and Allen Lemieux. Thanks also to Judy and Chad Ball.

Mary K. would like to give special thanks to her cousins Sandy and John Lowery of Applied Innovation whose contribution made this book possible. And to all the people, including anonymous donors, who made generous financial contributions, you made this project possible and allowed us to cover the costs of producing the book so more money will go to Kids' Food Basket. We are eternally grateful.

The Kids' Food Basket staff and board throughout the years have continued the work that Mary K. started, making the organization bigger and better and more comprehensive than seemed possible when they started as a small group of volunteers in a church basement. Bridget Clark Whitney has led the organization with compassion and expertise. Ashley Diersch, Christine Lentine, Kimberly Moore, Lisa Tamburello, Leah Hein, Hannah Grant, Aman Fox and Chelsi DeGennaro offered information and support from the beginning of the book writing process.

There are so many people who worked behind the scenes, who we thank for sharing their time and talents. Abby Holcolm used her amazing talents to design the cover. Mary Command served as friend and advisor. Michael Buck took Mary K.'s photograph. Dan Salas served as videographer for all the various promotions and website needs. Auden Rein designed the website and set it up. Joy Walczak joined the team to head up our promotion efforts. Jason Gillikin of Lakeshore Literary designed the book interior, published the book, and made sure Kids' Food Basket would benefit as much as possible financially. Accountants and lawyers who are friends of Mary K., including Jonathan Siebers and Anthony Pearson, Paul Toczydlowski and Lena Abissi set up the financial and legal systems for the book and helped facilitate donation of part of the proceeds to Kids' Food Basket.

We extend sincere gratitude to all the teachers, secretaries, and paraprofessionals who worked to assure students were given sack suppers without the stigma. They find creative solutions to do this and keep an eye out for the quiet souls in need. We also want to acknowledge all teachers everywhere for the work they do to overcome barriers to help students learn.

Lisa would like to acknowledge and thank her family, of course, her husband David Rein, and her kids, Auden Rein and Michol Rein, for showing her a life that is meaningful, and her mom, Rose Ley, for always believing she could do anything.

Mary K. would also like to acknowledge and thank her husband Jeff, her stepdaughter Mel and grandson JJ, her family and friends, and her parents, Marion and Tom Roach, for providing her the foundation in life that helped her face every obstacle with optimism and hope.

Dedication to Armen
George Oumedian
From Mary K. Hoodhood

Armen George Oumedian had the mind of an engineer, whether he was looking at machinery, organizations, or people. He was detail-oriented, analytical, and deeply curious. I suppose that is why he showed an interest in me, the sister of his son-in-law. If you were at dinner with Armen, he would make sure to include you in the conversation, and he would be genuinely absorbed in what you had to say. At family gatherings from the time I was a teenager into adulthood, he would talk with me about what I was doing and how life was going. He shared his own stories and over time became a true friend. After my injuries, he continued to be my friend and not only listened when I told him what I was doing, he showed up.

When I was volunteering at God's Kitchen, Armen and his wife Patricia would volunteer, too. They were deeply in love and really enjoyed spending time together in a way that was notable. Both Armen and Patricia were dedicated to family, friends, and community, which mirrored my own feelings and drew us together. After Armen retired, they used their resources to create the Armen G. and Patricia P. Oumedian Family Foundation to support causes they believed in. The list of organizations they helped is extensive.

Whatever Armen did, he was all in, which meant he not only gave money, but would become involved. If he had a philosophy of life, it was, "If you're going to get involved, don't just go halfway. Go all the way. It's always good to help, but if you really have a passion, let your passion flow. There will be bumps along the way, so work to smooth those bumps out."

Mary K. with Armen Oumedian.

When he and Patricia offered a scholarship for students from West Michigan to attend his alma mater, General Motors Institute (GMI), now Kettering University, they would plan gatherings for the students they sponsored. Armen and Patricia would take the students out to a nice restaurant and discuss their progress and the challenges they were facing. They also created The Armen Awards at Grand

Rapids Community College (GRCC) where they funded projects for students who developed programs for nonprofits. He would meet with the students and advise them on the projects, and he would meet with the professors to discuss what resources they needed. Of course, the students loved him. Everybody did. Armen would invite me to the final program when students presented their projects. It was inspiring to see all the commitment to community that Armen cultivated.

Armen and Patricia didn't start out affluent. They were first- and second-generation Americans. Armen's parents came to the United States from Armenia. His father was a woodworker who didn't speak English at first. His father built the popcorn wagon that I frequented at Michigan State University football games. Armen sold newspapers as a boy. Armen's parents worked and saved, and when they had a little extra, they would see a need in their community and share their savings. Patricia's family also came from modest means and worked hard.

They met at Union High School, where they hung around with the same group of friends. At first, they were dating other people, but soon started seeing each other. After high school, Armen enlisted in the army during World War II but was sent home after he was shot in the leg. He received a Purple Heart. He and Patricia got married in a surprise wedding. When Armen was to return to service, the war had ended. So, they started their family, having Pam, who married my brother Terry, followed by Kathey, and Dan.

Armen attended GRCC and GMI and became the engineer he was meant to be. He went to work at Rapistan, a materials handling firm, traveling to help companies develop plans for warehouses, airports, and other businesses. He retired at 70, but then a group of engineers started a new company, and he couldn't resist the excitement of a new challenge. He worked at Pinnacle Automation/Alvey until he retired again at 80.

When I approached him about a new program that I had started to feed kids who didn't have food at home, he was immediately interested. His initial donations made the organization and its future growth possible. Armen was a consistent helper, mentor, and supporter. He was so interesting and wonderful to talk to and a pure giver. We would go out to lunch or dinner and talk about nonprofits. He visited the church basement and looked at what we were doing. He always had helpful suggestions to make our process more efficient so we could serve more kids. For the first ten years, he and Patricia were involved. After her death in 2011, Armen continued to donate to and support Kids' Food Basket, allowing us to grow and improve our mission.

Armen wanted to be someone who had a positive impact on his community. I can truly say, "He made a difference." I am dedicating this book to Armen Oumedian because of his friendship and his example as a person who loved life and the people in his life. The support he gave me and the means to start Kids' Food Basket were just the icing on the cake.

APPENDIX A
KIDS' FOOD BASKET TIMELINE

Kids' Food Basket was founded to ensure access to nutritious, ready-to-eat meals for West Michigan children who are under-resourced and affected by poverty and food insecurity. The organization's mission is to nourish kids to reach their full potential, because healthy food is a right, not a privilege. As an independent 501(c)(3) nonprofit, Kids' Food Basket is community funded, which means every healthy meal is funded by donors.

2002 | **First Steps**

Founded in 2002, KFB operates in shared spaces with three small gifts of $1,000 and a pool of community volunteers. KFB begins serving 125 meals to three schools in Grand Rapids.

2005 | **A Home on Butterworth**

Due to the increasing need, Kids' Food Basket expands to a rented space on Butterworth Street in Grand Rapids with room to serve more children and respond to community requests. By engaging hundreds of volunteers and creating the Kids Helping Kids program, thousands of children now have consistent access to nourishing Sack Suppers.

2009 | 2,500 Students a Day

During the height of the 2009 recession, KFB grows to serve 2,500 students a day by implementing LEAN Six Sigma practices. A 1,900% increase from 2002!

2010 | New Home and National Recognition

To respond to a growing waiting list, KFB moves its headquarters to a rented space at 2055 Oak Industrial Drive. KFB receives national recognition by winning the Governor's Service Award for Volunteer Program of the Year, and founder Mary K. Hoodhood receives the Citizens Medal from President Barack Obama.

2012 | Muskegon Launches

KFB launches the Muskegon County program to respond to the one in four children in Muskegon who are food insecure. KFB is now serving 1,600 kids and counting!

2014 | Community Acknowledgment

Thanks to support from surrounding communities, KFB wins two significant awards: The Grand Rapids Area Chamber of Commerce EPIC Award for Nonprofit of the Year and MiBiz's Best Managed Nonprofit Award for Excellence in Fundraising.

2015 | Holland Launches

To better respond to the 11,120 children in Ottawa County who live with food insecurity, KFB expands to Ottawa County. Each weekday, this program currently serves 1,100 students across eight schools.

2016 | One Million Meals and Infinite Impact

As a result of a growing volunteer and donor community, KFB reaches the tremendous milestone of serving 1,000,000 healthy, nourishing meals in one school year in West Michigan. A new service school has a 21% increase in national test scores, which the principal attributes solely to receiving consistent healthy meals from KFB.

2017 | Last Farmland in Grand Rapids

The opening of the Kids' Food Basket Farm – Kent County, a chemical-free, sustainable 10-acre farm located in the heart of Grand Rapids. Now, delicious kid-tested, parent-approved vegetables and fruit are grown and harvested right on-site.

2019 | Permanent Kids' Food Basket Headquarters

KFB expands to its 30,000-square-foot LEED-certified headquarters on 1300 Plymouth Avenue NE, complete with 10 acres of sustainable farmland, a greenhouse and a learning barn. KFB is currently serving over 9,300 children and families in four counties, with the capacity to serve up to 15,000 meals a day and donate thousands of pounds of fresh produce to our community partners.

2020 | Ottawa + Allegan Expansion

KFB secures a permanent home at 652 Hastings Avenue in Holland to serve both Ottawa and Allegan counties. Thanks to the championship of local leadership and generous donors, this space allows KFB to service additional schools in need of healthy, life-affirming evening meals.

2021 | Ground Up Learning Lab Launches

Ground Up Learning Lab is a series of online, interactive lessons and activities for students and families. Lessons focus on community engagement, home gardening, sustainability and healthy lifestyle habits. GULL is a free curriculum that students, educators and parents can use to find a variety of resources to learn and grow together.

2022 | Kids' Food Basket Farm – Ottawa + Allegan Opens

KFB announces the development of a 10-acre sustainable, chemical-free farmland, a greenhouse and a learning barn in Ottawa County. The farm, a shared property in partnership with Ridge Point Community Church in Holland, will be used to increase food provision and expand our Grow commitment in Ottawa and Allegan counties. Produce grown on the newly acquired farmland will go directly into Sack Suppers and into the community to help increase access to healthy food for the residents of Ottawa and Allegan counties.

The information in this appendix is adapted from Kids' Food Basket's 20th anniversary timeline. Used with permission.

APPENDIX B
FOOD INSECURITY REPORT

T he State of Michigan conducted a study of food insecurity, published in February 2022. Three important highlights from this report bear repeating.

———

1. The social determinants of food insecurity have the greatest impact on the nature, scope, and causes of food insecurity. There is an interconnectedness between poverty, health, and food security.

These social determinants include racial and ethnic inequality; health, age, and disability status; and poverty, income, and unemployment status. There is often a perpetual cycle of income restriction, food insecurity, and adverse health outcomes which is incredibly difficult to break independently and highlights the necessity of federal, state, and charitable food assistance programs. The COVID-19 pandemic has exacerbated these challenges for those disparately vulnerable to food insecurity.

2. The cost of food insecurity is exorbitant, affecting health care, education, and productivity costs.

Michigan falls above the 75th percentile nationally for annual statewide healthcare costs associated with food insecurity, or $1,801,282,000 per year. COVID-19 pandemic-related healthcare costs were increased by the high numbers of patients with chronic disease, many of which are exacerbated by poor diet and nutrition. Educational costs, lost productivity, and lower lifetime earnings due to food insecurity bring Michigan's total "hunger bill" to $5.51 billion dollars per year.

3. Cost-effective policies that enhance federal and state food and nutrition programs, increase charitable food assistance, and clinically integrate food-as-medicine programs in health care have the potential to decrease food insecurity.

Federal and state food and nutrition programs, including SNAP, WIC, school meals, pandemic-related waivers and flexibilities to these programs, including Pandemic EBT (P-EBT) have demonstrated economic, educational, and health impacts. Charitable food distributions bring economic as well as other benefits to households, and to the economy. Clinically integrated food-as-medicine programs, from home-delivered groceries to produce prescriptions to medically tailored meals, show promise in reduced healthcare utilization costs and health outcomes, yet require sustainable funding to be effective for Michigan patients and for the economy in the long-term.

———

Read the whole report: https://www.michigan.gov/-/media/ Project/Websites/mdhhs/Folder2/FSC_Final_Report1.pdf? rev=a649563170a9477892c247f254e4dac2).

Appendix C
Donation Link

To support the efforts of Kids' Food Basket to nourish children, use the QR code below to donate.

Visit kidsfoodbasket.org for more information.

CPSIA information can be obtained
at www.ICGtesting.com
Printed in the USA
JSHW022232201222
35179JS00016B/31